Contemporary Catechetics Series

Prompted by many demands, a series of contributions to the "Writings on Catechetics" in the German publication, *Catechetical Papers*, now appear
in book form. Selected for inclusion are those articles and essays of a particularly catechetical nature. The completed series of books will mirror the
catechetical questions and problems of our day,
as they are extracted from the "Writings" of the
Catechetical Papers. Theoretical as well as practical themes will be chosen, in keeping with the aims
and purposes of the magazine itself. This contem-
plated series will include essays on the development
of new catechetical approaches, on the significance
of Israel in religious instruction, and on the new insights into the teachings about "the last things," as
well as on other pertinent catechetical issues.

FATHER JOSEF GOLDBRUNNER

Series Editor

ISRAEL

IN

CHRISTIAN RELIGIOUS

INSTRUCTION

☦

edited

by

THEODOR FILTHAUT

UNIVERSITY OF NOTRE DAME PRESS, 1965

Imprimi Potest:
> Howard J. Kenna, C.S.C.,
> Provincial

Nihil obstat:
> Joseph Hoffman, C.S.C.,
> Censor deputatus

Imprimatur:
> ✠ Leo A. Pursley, D.D.,
> Bishop of Fort Wayne-South Bend
> February 28, 1965

Original German title:

ISRAEL IN DER CHRISTLICHEN UNTERWEISUNG
First published by Kösel Verlag, Munich, 1963

INTRODUCTION

The collection of essays in this book originated largely from lectures given during a seminar on pastoral theology at the University of Münster in the 1961–1962 academic year. The purpose of the seminar was to study the theme, "The Jews in Christian Religious Instruction," as found in current catechetical literature. The selection of this theme was motivated by past experience in teaching salvation history: religious instruction was not giving adequate attention to the significance of Israel. The object of these lectures would have been lost if our research had extended into the history of catechetical tradition. Only in one essay, "The Jews in the *Roman Catechism*," was it necessary to deal with that tradition.

The aim of the seminar was to present the facts and to attempt to understand them. When it was later decided to make the findings available to the public, the lectures were re-edited for publication and enhanced in part by examples from practical teaching experience.

One aspect of these facts is the influence of literature on the student for whom it is intended. Therefore, the research deals not only with literary sources—catechisms, biblical text books and other supplementary reading—but also with the efficacy of such literature in the student's own world.

The contributions in this book, however, constitute only a beginning of a great task which can no longer be delayed. This applies expressly to my own chapter, "The Jews in Christian Religious Instruction," wherein I have attempted to indicate the structure for discussing the subject matter. The essayists themselves realize that their work is only a start. If their attempts will but help to stimulate thought on a truth all too long neglected, and to encourage profitable discussion about it in catechetical instruction, that effort has not been in vain.

Theodor Filthaut

CONTENTS

THE JEWS IN CHRISTIAN RELIGIOUS EDUCATION

Theodor Filthaut

Why the avoidance of this topic in catechetics?

There is a great similarity between the problems of how to treat the question of the Jews in catechetics and how to speak about the proper treatment of the different Christian religions. Much has been written in past years about the relationship of the Christian to the Jew and of the Catholic to the Protestant; but in catechetical literature, and consequently in catechetical practice, such issues are taboo. As a rule, the "Jewish question" is shunned both in catechetical and in biblical instruction, and even more so in Church history. The same may be said about preaching. In France, where Father Démann has labored in this field for many years, the situation is better than in the German-speaking countries. So far, the publications of the group associated with the *Freiburger Rundbrief* in Germany have had little effect. Apart from some laudable exceptions, neither preachers nor catechists have paid any attention to the *Rundbrief*. This is an astonishing and rather disquieting fact. Even though Pope John XXIII expressed his thinking on the Jews by revising a certain prayer in the Good Friday liturgy,[1] though the German bishops did not hesitate to speak up by way of their declarations on the Eichmann Trial and their requests for prayers on behalf of the Jews,[2] and though the German *Katholikentage* since 1945 have often taken a position in the matter,[3] preachers and catechists remained silent. At any rate, it is imperative today to be concerned about this task. Young people, in contrast to adults, are indeed interested in the problem to a great extent; at least, they are not adverse to being taught about it. Besides, the difficulties are not as likely to be found among them as among grown-ups. In the latter case, as far as it is at all feasible, interest in responsibility for the problem can be stimulated only after overcoming great initial resistance. It is not intended here to discuss whether, or how far, religious instruction and preaching have in the past contributed to the dreadful fate of the Jews. What is urgently needed is objectively historical and pastoral research into these problems. If nothing else, the present-day Jewish literature, which so often charges Christian religious instruction with the guilt of despising the Jews, should be reason enough to seriously begin scientific research into the matter. Anyone who even superficially touches upon catechetical literature from the viewpoint of the problem will readily recognize that religious instruction has not always

[1] Cf. Father Démann, "John XXIII and the Jews," in *Freiburger Rundbrief*, 45/48, 4–8.

[2] Cf. Father Démann, 50/52, 33.

[3] Cf. *Herder-Korrespondenz*, III (1948–1949), 45.

been imparted in the sense that Jesus Himself had taught about the Jews. That this should still be the case after 1945—that is, after all that has happened to the Jews in Germany during those preceding years—is clearly proved by checking the bibles, catechisms, and other supplementary reading materials used in schools. Furthermore, an investigation into the available literature of the last two centuries would indicate the same fact. What Father Démann[4] has shown to be true for the French-speaking countries can also be assumed to apply in a similar way to the German-speaking countries. But, as said before, the concern here is not with the historical deficiencies but only with the current teaching methods. What is actually at stake here is not only the objective teaching about Israel, but also the present situation, which is to develop a framework for this teaching. In order to avoid exaggerations and oversimplifications of this situation, a few remarks about terminology are in order.

It would hardly be proper in this discussion to treat "anti-Semitism," simply because we are not talking about Semites but about Jews. And we know well enough that these two terms are not quite the same. Who would not strongly and resentfully protest against being called an anti-Semite? This word has been overwrought through the past decades. But if we actually want to probe the thinking, feelings and values of our contemporaries, we need to

---

[4] Cf. Father Démann, *La catechèse chrétienne et le peuple de la bible* (Paris, 1952). See also *Herder-Korrespondenz,* VII (1952–1953), 312–315.

differentiate. We can better arrive at the truth by
distinguishing between hate, enmity, aversion, re-
vulsion or apathy toward the Jews on the one
hand, and despising, belittling or ridiculing on the
other. There is no doubt that these phenomena still
exist in our present society. And it is only for this
reason that the silence of preachers, educators and
parents can be understood.

Reasons for instruction about Israel

It is the job of religious instruction to teach the
word of God about Israel as well as to cultivate attitudes that correspond to these teachings. What are
the necessary conditions then for carrying out these
two specific tasks?

Above all, and quite simply, it is necessary to discuss the Jews in catechetical instruction. The truth
about Israel, to which the word of God is witness,
must neither be forgotten nor ignored in silence. It
needs to be brought to light and anchored in con-
ciousness. Most catechetical works of the past centuries have practically disregarded this truth and
therefore left it undisclosed. Unique, however, are
the catechetical works of Bishop Bernard Gula of
Brixen (1764–1856), who unlike any other catechetical writer in the German language, was quite aware
of the problem posed for Christians by the existence
of the Jews, and who had tried to represent it from
a deeply religious feeling of responsibility.

Why is it so important and so necessary to point
out that task—which should be self-explanatory—of
teaching the truth about Israel and not ignoring it

in silence? There are several reasons to prove this necessity.

The first reason is the widespread ignorance of what the Christian faith actually teaches about the Jews. What do Christians in general know about the characteristics and peculiarities of the Jewish faith? What do they know about the Jewish ritual of worship, the Jewish forms of piety, the connection between Synagogue and Church, or the ever-existing significance attached to Israel's salvation history? Who actually knows the facts about that fateful history of the relationship between Christians and Jews and not merely the one-sided truth that in the beginning the Jews persecuted Jesus? Who would go so far as to challenge the reality that such ignorance is actually rooted in inadequate instruction? An overwhelming proof for this contention can be found not only in our own experience, but also in the catechetical literature of the past and even of the present. How rarely has that problem been treated even in books, periodicals, or reference works which have appeared since 1945! Christian religious instruction simply must refrain from such silence, which still exists for unexplainable reasons. It might be well and very instructive to explore the reasons for that silence, but it is even more important to break through it and replace it with an instruction which is thorough and takes into account the richness of the testimony of faith.

The second reason leads us into a field where instruction is faced with an even more arduous task than in the first. We are confronted not only with insufficient knowledge about the Jews but also with much that is outrightly wrong. This area covers more than merely certain prejudices and generalizations that degradingly characterize the Jews; rather it involves the often mistaken religious concepts that have estranged many Christians and made it impossible for them to conceive the situation of the Jews. Since these concepts have been passed on traditionally from generation to generation and, in addition, appear under the guise of biblical truths, they have influenced in a strong and deadly manner both the consciousness as well as the unconsciousness of the faithful. The ideas that the curse of God is the fate of the Jewish people and that their dispersal throughout the world is a just punishment for their killing of Jesus Christ— these and many other misconceptions—are like a wall between the faithful of the New Testament and those of the Old Testament, preventing the former to see the real vocation of the latter in Israel.

Connected with their prejudices and concepts so contrary to the truth are anti-Jewish attitudes and resentments, which demand a doctrine that would adhere to the truth. Whoever believes that such attitudes exist only among so-called anti-Semites is being perditiously deceived. Public opinion polls taken since 1945 prove the contrary. Nevertheless it should hardly be a matter of indifference to our Christian educators that there is still an influx of subconscious feelings which are contrary to the present mentality. For a day may come again when such anti-Jewish attitudes might form the psychological basis for recurrence of the past horrible experiences.

Significant as these reasons may be, we have not yet mentioned the most important motivation. For this problem is above all a question of the integrity of Christian belief. The wrong consciousness and the mistaken behavior of Christians concerning Jews constitute not only an injustice against them but also a misdeed against one's own belief. The fate of the Jewish people is intrinsically interwoven into salvation history which forms the object of belief. Neither the history of the Old Testament nor of the New until the fulfillment of all things through the Second Coming of Christ can be taught adequately without consideration of the role played by the Jewish people according to the will of God. In addition, it is part of the doctrine of Christian life that the acceptance of the Jewish people be included. Therefore, both the integrity and the fullness of the Christian faith forbid such exclusion of God's chosen people of the Old Testament in preaching and teaching.

What is a Jew?

Since more than one reason has been established for the need of pointing out the significance of the Jews in salvation history and of proceeding to a kind of instruction that embodies the word and the spirit of the gospels, we must now ask ourselves what is meant by teaching what faith teaches. The following is an attempt to present a few practical rules for religious instruction. As far as the prac-

tice of preaching and catechesis is concerned, we
still need a reliable theological interpretation of
Israel's mission in salvation history, an interpretation which does not omit anything that revelation
testifies about it. Many fine attempts at such interpretation have already been made, and we must
continue to develop these beginnings into a theological treatise. But, on the practical side, we cannot wait until the science of theology is ready to
offer such a mature doctrine. We must solve the
task, to the best of our ability, even today. Let us
then consider some of the essential points of such
instruction.

First, and above all, we have the task of handing
down a proper understanding of "the Jew." Beyond
the discriminatory collective concept, on the one
hand, and the vague generalizations, on the other,
we must teach the understanding of the Jews as
the one people chosen and called by God in the Old
Testament. The question, "Who and what is a Jew?"
has to be answered clearly, and such an answer
must have its roots in faith. The special characteristics and traits of the Jewish person can be determined only from the viewpoint of membership as
mentioned above. Our answer, therefore, involves
the Jewish faith. This faith consists of obedient
acceptance and observance of the word of the living God as proclaimed by the Law and the prophets.
It has to be placed into the context of both the
Christian faith and the manifold forms of pagan
belief. The relationship between the Jewish and
the Christian belief must not, however, be contem

plated only from the point of view of divergence
and opposition. At the moment, there does not
seem to be any reason to believe that this divergence, which exists essentially in the belief that
Jesus of Nazareth is the Messiah, will disappear.
Yet we have reason to denote that there is also a
sense of community in the act of faith as well as in
the content of faith. Even if belief in Jesus as the
Christ separates Christians and Jews, they are both
united in the acceptance of the Revelation given in
the Old Testament. This common ground distin-
guishes both the Jew and Christian from any pagan. Since our understanding of such a common
tie is only faintly being developed, and possibly
does not even exist, it is becoming nevertheless one
of the foremost postulates of present-day instruction about Israel. An example signifying that catechesis of the past had not altogether neglected
this aspect is given us by Bishop Galura, whom we
have already mentioned and who is known as the
foremost writer of catechetical literature in his
time. Upon reading his *Biblical History of the Redemption of the World through Jesus, the Son of
God,*[5] or his six volumes of *Newest Theology of
Christianity,*[6] one is struck with the frequency of
his concern about the significance of the Jews for
salvation history. He is also concerned about an
understanding of the Jews rooted in Holy Scripture,
which he uses as an educational basis for developing Christian attitudes. In the first-mentioned work

[5] Augsburg, 1806.
[6] Augsburg, 1800–1804.

is found the following text which can hardly be matched by anything in catechetical literature:

Who are these Jewish people? The original people of God, the first children and heirs of the heavenly Father and His celestial kingdom. If religion is likened to a tree, the Jews are the first, natural branches and twigs of this holy tree, which the Heavenly Father has cultivated with great care and love: the Jews are the door through which, and the bridge over which, mankind enters the kingdom of God. Children, do not despise the Jews but pity them; for salvation comes from the Jews, and they have suffered much for your sake.[7]

The distinguishing marks of Bishop Galura are not only his unusual interest in and irenic concept of the Jewish people, but also his efforts to write about this subject so copiously. In that area, he stands out noticeably among the catechetical writers of the past as well as today.

The tasks outlined here consist largely of awakening the proper understanding of the existence of the Jews. Is it really necessary to point out that such understanding has nothing in common with a tendency to belittle or destroy the difference in a belief which springs from a mistaken tolerance? In addition, concern about proper understanding must be coupled with a vigorous rejection of over-all collective discrimination against and a superficial judgment of the Jews. The often expressed opinion

[7] *Op. cit.*, 186; cf. also his other book, Vol. IV, 263–264.

that such an outright rejection is not necessary
seems to be illusory. The baseless and somewhat
malicious generalizations, which, unfortunately, are
still so obvious that they need not even be mentioned, can yet be found, not only in the jargon of
"anti-Semitism," but also, though in modified form,
in the very methods of Christian proclamation and
instruction. Such traditional methods can even be
detected in the sermons of St. John Chrysostom,[8]
who died in 407. It is disadvantageous to this task
of enlightening our consciousness when we occasionally express collective judgments and evalua-
tions that tend toward the opposite. Opinions that
see the Jewish people as chosen by God on the
basis of their ethical qualities, or that judge the
Jews only on grounds of their faithfulness to God,
are not only unacceptable but also quite objection-
able, because they may lead to a further obdura-
tion of the opposite extreme. It may well be that
such unwarranted glorification of the Jewish people is hindering rather than furthering many pro-
Jewish currents which had sprung up since 1945.
Christian instruction need not serve either the deg-
radation or the idealization of the Jewish people.
There are good Jews and bad Jews, just as among

[8] Compare the judgment of K. H. Schelkle in his study,
"Kirche und Synagogue in der frühen Auslegung des
Römerbriefes," which says: "Even in St. Chrysostom's
polemic against the Jews we can notice how an extremely
fanatical hatred harms the relationship between Church and
Synagogue." And further: "For St. Chrysostom, it is always
the Jews who are at fault; they are arrogant, imprudent,
quarrelsome and obnoxious." *Theol. Quartalschrift* (1945),
317 f.

any other people. Holy Scripture, both in the Old
and New Testaments, bear this out on many occasions. Factual instruction about the Jews should
avoid all generalization and any prejudgment; it
should not sit in judgment over the ethical advan-
tages or defects of individuals or whole groups, but
rather it must defend the Jews against unjust and
prejudiced representation. Even more important is
the need of positive teaching about the unique dignity which the Jewish person possesses as a member of the people of the Covenant.

Catechesis concerning the Old Testament and present-day Israel

Thus we arrive at the second task of religious
instruction. Understanding of the Jewish person can
be reached only on the basis, and through the history, of Israel. Without at least elementary knowledge of the history of this people, instruction about
the Jewish person remains abstract, vague and
ineffective. Only from a historical standpoint will
the truth about the Jew—that he is a member of
Israel—gain depth and plausibility. And only in this
way can the true understanding and respect for
the Jewish people be effected. Hence a careful
treatment in instruction—one without apathy, of
course—is a requisite. The various and manifold
happenings of the Old Testament are to be understood as parts of the great history of Israel's being
chosen and being called. Nowadays it is generally
accepted in catechetical circles that the history of
the Old Testament is not to be interpreted as an

arsenal of exemplified virtue, but simply as God's history for the salvation of mankind. Above all, the fact must never be overlooked that it is the history of God with the very people of Israel whose living descendants are the same Jews of today. Therefore, today's Jews are to be seen as the offspring of Abraham and the other patriarchs, as members of a people founded by Moses and a people that can count upon the prophets as their greatest witnesses for revelation. Thus grounded in historical truth, catechesis can only then paint the true and full picture of the Jewish person. The aim of such instruction is not to seek mere knowledge about the past but rather develop an understanding of the present.

In order to reach this goal then, the catechumen must essentially conceive the idea of the Jew as a member of a people carrying the burden of a great responsibility, which, in contrast to all other peoples, finds itself uniquely close—a closeness founded by God Himself—to the members of the New Testament, the Christians.

The connection between the Old and New Testaments

Another task required of catechetical instruction is that of establishing the connection which exists between the Old and the New Testaments. The outstanding factor in this connection should be the truth that it was the one same God who spoke through His prophets and through His Son (cf. Heb. 1:1–2). Among preachers and catechists, there prevails a trend toward praising the New Testament in favor of the Old. The Old Testament is more often presented as a religion of fear and trembling, whereas the New Testament is contrasted as the religion of love and joy. The same kind of misrepresentation and simplification occurs when the God of justice is contrasted with the God of grace, or the fear-inspiring king contrasted with the loving father. As a parallel to such contrasting concepts there is the confrontation of the Jews' outward and legalistic piety (to the letter) and the Christians' inner and "truly heartfelt" piety. These and similar interpretations should be stopped and replaced by the explanation that the New Covenant did not need a degrading or discrediting of the Old. Such black-and-white representations are much preferred on account of their psychological effects. There seems to be but one remedy for the dangerous effects of misrepresentations: unbiased reading of the scriptures of both the Old and the New Testaments. Recognition, not only of the differences but of the common aspects, will be the fruit of such study. There are not two different salvation histories, but only one history of God and man, which started in the Old Testament and is brought to completion in the New. The coming of the kingdom of God, of the King and Father of men, is at the same time the central event as well as the great and all-embracing theme of this one history. Since only differences dominate our present-day consciousness, it behooves us—not only as a matter of justice toward the Jews but also toward the acts of God in the

ime before Jesus Christ—to bring out of oblivion
he things we have in common. In this instance we
:annot specifically describe the full context of what
ve do have in common, although the common be-
ief of Jews and Christians in the revelation of the
)ne and only God in the history of Israel contains
nuch of this context. Let us at least point out the
ollowing facts: the seam between the Old and the
New Testaments is the figure and the life of Jesus
Christ. It is of extreme importance in the catechet-
cal portrayal of this connection to teach emphat-
cally the fact that Jesus came "from Nazareth"
ınd descended from the house of David; that Mary
ınd Joseph, the Apostles and disciples, and Christ
Himself were all Jews, namely, members of Israel,
leeply tied to the history of their people. Further-
nore, a catechist should make quite clear the significance of the fact that the whole life and work
)f Jesus, the founder of the New Covenant, was
:nacted within the borders of Israel. Even before
His death He kept the Pasch with His Apostles. To
:xplain that Christ's own flesh and blood came from
he Jewish people and that He kept a conscious
:ense of community with them—He never aban-
loned them in spite of His battle against their un-
)elief—can produce wholesome and fruitful results,
f the concrete details are presented vividly and
:ffectively. A prerequisite for such an effect, how-
:ver, is a completely unbiased representation of
he happenings that show Jesus' relationship to His
)eople, and this process should then deny any
:apacity for differentiation.

Christ's passion and the
anti-Jewish attitude

It is above all Christ's passion that needs to be presented in such light, for the death of Christ, even today, is still among Christians the main source of anti-Jewish feelings. In fateful simplification, "the Jews" are charged with "deicide." They are therefore "the bad Jews," the "murderers of God," who must live under His curse from the time of Jesus' death. In this inconceivably calloused way their hard fate, which in the course of centuries caused them so much suffering and persecution, is considered the just punishment of God. This is a truly fearful paradox: Christ's death at Golgotha suffered for the redemption of all men, but especially for the chosen people, has become the motive for the condemnation of the whole chosen people—the sign of divine love having become the reason for hate. Of all misunderstandings that most need to be clarified when proclaiming the Christian message, it is the one about the cross. Here lies a most gratifying task that will bear much fruit. All that is needed is factual and just representation. But this type of representation requires the art of differentiation. It is necessary to draw a clear line between the people of Israel at the time of Christ and those groups who actually were at fault in causing the death of Christ; to make sure that the role played by "the heroes"— Pilate and his soldiers—is not forgotten; to reiterate that the Jews of later generations should never be identified with their coreligionists of those times;

nd lastly—even more important than these hap-
enings on the surface of history, even if belonging
o another historical dimension—it is necessary to
each that truth is not silenced, and that the true
nd actual reason for the death of the Redeemer is
he sin and guilt of every human being.

he history of the relation
etween Church and Synagogue.

Another point needing clarification is the history
f the relationship between Church and Synagogue.
his history encompasses the time from the begin-
ings of the Church through the centuries down to
ur own days. Reference to the earliest period is
he one that carries the most weight. The Church
Jesus Christ is "the Church of Jews and pagans."
is against all historical fact to so depict the
gins of the Church as to create the impression
at the Church, unlike the Synagogue, consisted
ily of non-Jewish persons. Contrariwise, we are
ity-bound to make clear that according to Christ's
ords "salvation came from the Jews" (John 4:22),
d that the Church in her original make-up, as
ell as in her highest dignitaries (the "Twelve,"
Cor. 15:5), consisted of members of the Jewish
ople. It is well known that in His proclamation
sus had addressed only the Jews. In her begin-
ngs the Church was accustomed to proclaim the
essage of salvation to "the sons of the House of
rael." That is why St. Paul in his travels visited the
nagogues and preached to the Jews so as to win
em over to the faith of Jesus, the Messiah, as an-

nounced in Holy Scripture (Acts 13:5, 14:14 ff.)
Only later did Paul begin proclaiming the Christia
message to the non-Jews, the pagans. The history c
the Apostles contains a treasure of material to illus
trate in catechetical instruction this early relation
ship between Church and Synagogue. How fa
removed we are in our present-day Christian con
sciousness from this vital truth that the proclama
tion of the gospel by Jesus Christ and the Apostle
had taken place to great extent within the Jewis
worship service itself! What vistas of change woul
open up if Christians and Jews again would nc
only recognize this historical truth but acknowledg
it! Moreover, this historical truth is a testimon
that the early Christians did have a living know
edge of their connection with Israel in salvatic
history and that they were quite conscious of the
responsibility toward their brethren of Israel. I
H. Schelkle, in his article already cited, writes the
about it:

Synagogue and Church—this is the summation c
the early exegesis of the Epistle to the Romans
are still united in the beginning with each othe
in their knowledge of common salvation; in the
constantly living hope of a community of fai
still to be attained; and finally in their innermo
expectation of salvation. In spite of all enmit
they are tied to each other in this.[9]

After those first centuries this relationsh
changed so much that, from then on, the Chur
and Synagogue considered themselves as two re

[9] *Op. cit.*, 316.

gions estranged from, and opposed to, each other. Their separation became an established fact.[10]

All ensuing history of the relationship between Church and Synagogue, right up to our own days, has been influenced by the mutual consciousness of this complete separation. Not all the chapters of this history have yet been written, but the results now available to historical research unfortunately bare too much of the shameful and the regrettable that the Jews had suffered from the hands of the Christians.[11] Even though the black-and-white presentation is not always justified—a presentation which has nothing to do with reality and which is often featured in novels and popularizations—there is no contesting the fact that the pages of that history should fill the Christian consciousness with shame and remorse. It is an injustice for text books in Church history to record that the Christians were persecuted by the Jews during the first centuries, but to remain silent on what the Christians had later done to the Jews by way of persecutions, expulsions, forced baptism, calumnies about ritual murder, desecration of the host, poisoning of wells, and other condemnable actions. [12] Quite apart from

[10] *Ibid.*, 317 f.
[11] Cf. the volumes: W. D. Marsch and K. Thieme, eds., 'Christen und Juden. Ihr Gegenüber vom Apostelkonzil bis heute" (1961).
[12] We hope that the case of A. Heuser, who admits the wrong on the part of the Christians as regards the Jews—which has made dialogue more difficult—will not remain an isolated incident. He makes it clear in his *Kirchengeschichte für den katholischen Religionsunterricht an Volksschulen Church History for Catholic Religious Instruction in Grade schools/* (1930), p. 70.

the fact that it is a matter of truth and justice, an elementary knowledge of this history is so very important because it will take the wind out of the sails of apathy and self-righteousness as regards the fate of the Jewish people. Such ignorance of the historical facts is partly to blame for the lagging interest and poor intention on the part of educators in treating the Jewish problem. It is, of course, a basic condition that the treatment of these things in religious instruction be practical and educationally acceptable. Therefore, religious instruction must be free of the pious rendering of facts as harmless and of exaggerated self-incrimination. There is no doubt that the relations between Christians and Jews knew periods of peaceful coexistence; certainly, Bernard of Clairvaux, Pius XII and John XXIII are not the only churchmen who have proved themselves helpers and friends of the Jews. Another valuable goal to keep in mind is awareness of the fact that the Church still has the mission of winning the Jews, as members of the Old Covenant, to faith in Jesus Christ. Obviously more and more Christians are becoming aware of this vital fact and are ready to serve it.

Fortunately, the history of the relationship between Church and Synagogue also saw times when both were able to meet in peaceful and fruitful ways. Such encounter, however, did not take place in the political, social or cultural sphere, but has been active through all the centuries in a quiet but efficient process. The liturgy as the core of the life of the Church, though essentially founded by Jesus

Christ, is in many parts based on the Old Testament. The scriptures of the Old Testament are widely used in the liturgy. And many a feast of the liturgical year has its prototype in the Old Testament; we need hardly be reminded of the two greatest Church seasons, Easter and Pentecost. In the sacraments, too, one way or another, similar connections can be found, particularly in the Holy Eucharist, which of course was prefigured in the paschal celebration and the sacrificial victims of the Old Testament. The fact that the psalms form the official prayerbook for both Jews and Christians further confirms the connection, not only between the Old and the New Testaments but also between the Church and the Synagogue in the early days. If, in addition, the faithful were to increase their veneration of the patriarchs and prophets, especially of Abraham, "the father of all them that believe" (Rom. 4:11)—which does have its rightful place in the liturgy, but has been vastly neglected to the point of naught in the consciousness of Christians over the centuries—it would serve as a means for rapprochement.

The Christian hope and the final liberation of Israel

The history of the relations between Church and Synagogue will last until the Second Coming of Christ. Until then it is the task of the Church to wait for the Jews and to win them over, not for reasons of human desire to rule but for the sake of their salvation. According to the Apostle Paul this

action of the Church will be accomplished just be
fore the Second Coming, for "all Israel should b
saved" (Rom. 11:26).[13]

Among the many things which come to mind i
attempting to think about "the Jewish question" i
the problem that, right up to our own times, cate
chetical literature makes very little mention of thi
fact of the final salvation of Israel. And yet the ex
pectation of their salvation is a considerable par
of Christian hope. One of many such testimonies o
this expectation can be cited from the old, remark
able text of the *Catechismus Catholicus,* by Bisho
Michael Helding of Merseburg (1506–1561):

> We should desire to see the day when the Jewis
> or Israelite people—still partially kept in dar
> ness—will be enlightened by divine grace to re
> ognize the salvation which Christ is offering
> the whole world, so that in the fullness of time
> the pagans the Jews can also be saved, as it
> written: "From Sion will come he who will tak
> away and prevent godlessness from Jacob."[14]

At this point we would like to mention a textboo
for high school students, a church history by
Heuser, which in its closing chapter does not e
clude teachings about the Second Coming of Chri
and the conversion of Israel. The truth of the gre
promise of God concerning the fate of the Jews

[13] In order to understand Chapters 9 to 11 of Romans,
important for an understanding of Israel's salvation, s
F. W. Maier, "Israel in der Heilsgeschichte," *Biblisc
Zeitfragen,* XII, (Münster, 1929), 11–12.

[14] Cologne (1562), 17.

within the content of faith and forms a part of the
teachings of the Second Coming. Such instruction,
therefore, that does not take into account the future
of Israel is incomplete. It is not easy to compre-
hend the paradox: that ignorance among the members of the new Israel should be so widespread that
the current interest in the anticipated union of the
two would assume the character of a novelty. And
yet, measured against its true meaning, such anticipation should be for the new Israel an occasion
for rejoicing and for deep consolation. Instruction
about this great promise has a twofold aim: to
spread the right kind of knowledge as well as to in-
still a living hope. A most gratifying result of such
instruction will be the eradication from the Christian consciousness of that erroneous concept of the
eternal damnation of the Jews—and thus no more
reason for the so-called superiority over Israel.

Christian charity and the Jewish person

Our considerations so far have been concerned
with the problem of proper instruction in regard to
Israel. It is, however, contrary to Christian teaching to be content only with the enlightenment of
our consciousness. As always, and in this matter
too, Christian education aims toward preparation
for leading a good life. In other words, and quite in
keeping with our problem, young people must be
educated so as to live their faith when it comes
to accepting the Jewish person. For it is actually
faith that worketh by charity" (Gal. 5:6) which is

at stake here. Nor does the commandment of neigh-
borly love, to which the Christian is committed,
permit any limitations. If *every* man must be loved,
that commandment ought to be even more effective in relation to the very people from whom
Christ was born and whom He has always loved in
a special way. The example for the Christian attitude toward the Jew is therefore Jesus' love for
His people. And if education seeks an example
among Christ's disciples, we might point to Paul
who could say of himself: "I speak the truth in
Christ, I lie not, my conscience bearing me witness
in the Holy Ghost: That I have great sadness, and
continual sorrow in my heart. For I wished myself
to be an anathema from Christ, for my brethren,
who are my kinsmen according to the flesh" (Rom.
9:1–3). Since a Christian's love springs from his
faith, it is of course motivated by other reasons
than ordinary natural love. It is therefore not a
mere superficiality to point to the essential differences, in view of the current interworldly motives
prevalent in the ethical attitude toward the Jews.

According to the Christian faith a Jew should
be loved not simply because, as commonly heard
"the Jews are also people." Love, based on faith
does not nullify this attitude but rather deepens it
quality. Moreover, such love is directed toward the
Jew as a person singled out by God's love, though he
has not as yet recognized, it is true, the coming of
the Messiah; a person to whom the message of His
coming must be preached again and again; and a
person in whom the word of promise of final salva-

tion will one day be accomplished. Also, such love has its origin in the attitude of God Himself toward Israel, as well as in God's specific commandment to love all men. To come back once more to Bishop Galura: "The contempt for the Jews, through whose faith we ourselves have gone into the kingdom of God, is unbiblical, un-Christian and ungrateful—and not at all the intention of God who has always loved Israel."[15]

Thus, true charity will not allow the Christian to support any anti-Jewish attitudes or mass-suggestions. Christian love rather obliges him to strive for justice, understanding and good will. Nor does charity embrace a spineless indifference to the defects and shortcomings of the Jewish people; instead it realizes that not only hate itself but also a sense of apathy is opposite to love. In the latter respect, the Christian community leaves much to be compensated. Expression of charity toward the Jews should be concerned with the following: authentic instruction about them; the proclamation of Christ's message to them with patience rather than overzealousness; prayers on their behalf; works of justice and respect; interest in their salvation; and finally with the happy expectation of their future fulfillment. Christian love is a creative force—a force that not only avoids evil, but realizes the good. Hence not saying anything against the Jews satisfies love no less than saying nothing in their favor. Silence about the Jews, therefore, certainly is no expression of love. The same can be said of

[15] Galura, *Neueste Theologie des Christenthumes,* IV, 186.

apathy and indifference toward the still-existing contempt of the Jews. All the feelings and aspects touched upon here take the shape of this one demand: to impart truthful knowledge and to educate so as to develop attitudes based on Christian love. The two are fundamentally but one task. To dedicate oneself to this challenging task today means to confront a kind of work that is not only urgent but also full of promise.

THE JEWS IN THE LITURGY

Gerhard Teske

1. Characteristics and Aims of Liturgical Instruction.

Liturgical instruction concerns itself with the liturgy of the Church, its forms, and content. Such instruction aims to create a foundation for the understanding of the liturgy—an understanding essential to the perceptive and faithful exercise of the liturgical functions. Such instruction further serves as a preparation for the actual celebration of the liturgy by the community. Acquaintance with the liturgy begins at home with the parents' instruction, continues during kindergarten and school years, and then develops by religious instruction of youth and the pastoral care of adults. Without such constant instruction from early youth, the liturgy will remain incomprehensible and the worshiping community will never advance beyond the role of passive spectators at the liturgical functions. A treasure which is not dug out and brought to light will remain hidden and unknown.

The recently accomplished liturgical renewal has indeed increased the awareness on the part of the faithful—quite common in the Church—that the liturgy is the high point of Christian faith and life. Since *lex orandi* is also, and in special measure, *lex credendi,* liturgical instruction parallels instruction in Christian faith and action. The Church expresses her faith in prayers, readings, and actions. Thus liturgy is also proclamation. And liturgical instruction serves Christian faith and action. In the treatment of this topic it will certainly be of great value to strive toward an understanding of the Jewish faith and to promote the right Christian attitude toward the Jews on the basis of what the liturgy teaches.

2. *The Jews in the Liturgy of the Church.*

First it is important to examine the liturgy in relation to Judaism so as to obtain material for liturgical instruction. Above all, this involves the connection not only between the Old and New Testaments, but also between the Church and the Synagogue. The Old Testament in the liturgy, along with its Jewish characteristics, is not simply a historically conditioned shell or frame with a new content, which can be arbitrarily changed or abolished, but rather an expression of the unity between the Jewish and Christian religions in the content of faith as well as in the many forms of worship. The Old Testament makes clear the unity of salvation history and with it the close ties between the people of the New Covenant and the people of the Old, which ties will continue to exist at all times. It is then only that liturgical instruction can effectively present the opportunity—not yet sufficiently exploited—to counteract the attitudes of estrangement that Chris-

ian circles harbor in regard to the Jews. Apart from
a hostility that finds its origin in racial discrimina-
ion against the Jews—which is still latent in spite
of the official condemnation of "anti-Semitism" and
anti-Jewish programs in recent history—the Old
Testament, though a part of the Holy Scripture of
the Church, is frequently considered something un-
important and outmoded, even in Christian circles.
Whenever it is treated in religious instruction, it is
more than likely presented as a collection of pious
and devotional stories, so that some incidents are
hardly comprehensible according to the present
ethical code. These become then "typically Jewish."

Even more effective than the Bible, the liturgy, in proclaiming the Christian message, brings
to the fore salvation history by grouping and inter-
preting the texts according to Old Testament norms,
and uses Jewish prayer texts for the conclusion of
the liturgical celebration. This is pointedly illustrated in the readings for the Lenten season and
by the use of Old Testament psalms and canticles.
In view of the fact that the recent effort on behalf
of Christian unity has found such strong support for
the liturgical movement among the various Christian creeds, it can be safely assumed that a more
profound understanding of the liturgy has made
Christians much more open toward an encounter
with Israel. Thus liturgical instruction appropriates
an important role in the "Jewish question." Therefore, we offer the following as suggestions for liturgical instruction.

3. *The Heritage of the Synagogue in the Liturgical Year.*

Liturgical instruction is best imparted when co ordinated with the events of the Church year "*Where* do we stand in the Church year?" is a question to be asked repeatedly in liturgical instruc tion, particularly at such times as the beginning o the school year, the beginning of a Church seasor or when there is a change in liturgical colors, an so forth. This, of course, not only applies to instruc tion at school but also to that in the home; to in struction of servers, commentators, the choir a Mass; to announcements in Church bulletins and t Christian doctrine. But it would be better not to fo low too closely the systematic instructions given a school. A catechist should insist upon the readin of specific passages and prayers from the miss for a deeper understanding of the liturgy on Sur days and major feasts. This also refers to th hymns of the specific cycles in the Church yea to the mode of celebration in Church, to the custom at home and in church, and so on. All this is a pre requisite in the present plans for school instructior

The Easter Cycle

The Easter cycle is the greatest, and historical the oldest, liturgical season. Even though in Chri everything is re-created and the fullness of tim has started, the Old Testament is everywhere er countered in the liturgy. The Old Testament an Judaism must be seen in close alliance here, esp cially since the Jews even today belong to the "Ol

Covenant" and are still expecting the fulfillment of
the promise. The fact that there are also nonortho-
dox and liberals among the "Jews" of today seems
to constitute a parallel with "Christians."

Today, with the renewal of the Easter liturgy,
every pastor will concentrate on Lent in a special
way. The new rubrics of recent years underline the
distinctive character of the daily Lenten Masses to
such an extent that in most of the ferial days it is
no longer feasible to deviate from the prescribed
liturgy by honoring a saint's feast. Nor can any of
the great number of readings from the Old Testament be omitted during that time, and these are
encountered every day of Lent without fail. They
are to be proclaimed to the community along with
the gospel in every service, even though it is per-
missible to shorten passages here and there to make
them more readily understandable. Emphasis on
the proper questions during religious instruction
and in the indispensable use of homilies during
Mass in Lent help to clarify through the Old Testament texts the mysteries of redemption. Such
deeper understanding of salvation history in the
Old Testament also may keep Christians from al-
ienating themselves from the Jews or rejecting
them, and can bridge the gap between the two religions, both of which use the same Holy Scriptures.
The works of Pius Parsch[1] and those of J. Pinsk[2]
are a great help in this direction.

---

[1] *The Church Year of Grace,* 5 vols. (Collegeville, Minn.,
The Liturgical Press, 1953–1959).

[2] "Das Pascha des Herrn, Quadragesima und Pentecostes,"
Liturgisches Leben (1934), fasc. 2.

Holy Week will always remain the high point o
all liturgical celebration, and consequently also o
liturgical instruction for children as well as adults
With careful preparation and direction, participa
tion in this supreme liturgical celebration of the
year may become a kind of strong tradition, a
least with a part of the community, just as it i
in many places with Midnight Mass at Christmas
the Corpus Christi procession, rogation days, pil
grimages, and others. Opinions vary about the fea
sibility of including children in these Holy Weel
celebrations, but for one thing children should cer
tainly not be excluded from the Palm Sunday pro
cession. Furthermore, there is no doubt that chil
dren experience a great joy during the services on
Holy Thursday and Good Friday, and especially a
the celebration of the Easter Vigil; this and the im
portant fact that early habits are formed here fo
life are a great factor in favor of encouraging chil
dren to participate.

The fact that the Christian Easter celebration i
rooted in the Jewish paschal celebration is clear
even the Christian calendar is patterned after the
Jewish one. Then, too, the word designated by the
Church for Easter, "Passover"—which Latin the
ology has translated into "transitus," that is, the
passage of Christ and Christianity from death to
life—belongs to the vocabulary of Judaism.

How peculiar is the fact that the Palm Sunda
procession at the start of Holy Week, in its outward
form as well as in its hymns, is nothing other than
an imitation of the acclaim which the Jews at tha

me offered to the "Son of David" in Jerusalem.
or comparison, note the antiphons during the dis-
ibution of the palms and the procession; note also
ie hymn sung during the procession.

The Last Supper shows the "Passover" character
ery clearly. The procedure at the "farewell super" was truly based on the ritual of the Jewish
assover celebration. Even this fact should not be
eated lightly in a simplified representation of the
ast Supper, as so often happens, one which sepa-
tes the meal from the Old Testament Passover
remony. Jesus ordered everything prepared ac-
rding to custom, corresponding to the festival
der. The loaves of unleavened bread, the offering
four cups of wine, the bitter herbs, the blessings
er the wine and meal, the sacrifice and the eat-
g of the paschal lamb, the Hallel psalms—all this
elonged to the last supper with Christ. The pious
ews even today keep their Passover in the same
anner by celebrating the *seder*.[3]

In the epistle of Easter Sunday, St. Paul refers
the Jewish custom of unleavened bread and the
aschal lamb. The designation of Christ as the
amb of God which is so familiar to us can only be
plained as originating in the Old Testament—see
e *Agnus Dei* of the Mass, the *Ecce Agnus Dei*
fore the second elevation, and so on. Another
teworthy reference is contained in the Second
esson of Good Friday from Exodus, and also the
aster Preface.

[3] Cf. Blumenfeld, I, *Pessach-Buch 5706–1946* (Marburg,
46).

The reading of the Passion according to the fou evangelists also contains an account of the part th Jewish people had experienced in the life and dea of Christ. But the Passion must not become th cause for heaping hot coals upon the heads of th Jews. Sin and men's faithlessness are overshad owed by the magnitude of Jesus Christ's lovin deed. There were Jewish people, too, who stood believers at the foot of the cross. Simon of Cyren and the women at the crossroads were of the sam blood. Jesus prays openly for His enemies and fo gives the two thieves at His side. The Church as th representative of Christ in the world must nev act or teach differently. The prayer for the Jew on Good Friday is directed toward the salvation this people. "Let us also pray for the Jews that o God and Lord will lift the veil from their hearts that they may also acknowledge our Lord Jes Christ. Almighty and eternal God, do not refu mercy even to the Jews. Hear our prayers. . . This prayer apparently parallels the one for th conversion of non-Christians. Should the Jew therefore, not be worthy of the same prayer that for the pagans? There is no denying that Chr tians have drawn a line here, perhaps inadve ently, but perhaps too because of being condition by the one-sided Christian teaching of the past.

The omission of the genuflection during the pray for the conversion of the Jews, as was the custc before the restoration of the Good Friday liturgy 1955, has anti-Jewish origins, as J. Henning prov in his article "The Place of the Jews in the Liturgy

4 *Liturgisches Jahrbuch (1960)*, Vol. 3.

According to his analysis, the accepted explanation for omitting the genuflection is not historically determined, because, according to St. Matthew (27:29) and St. Mark (15:19), it was not the Jews but the Romans who genuflected mockingly before Christ. Henning states: "The novelty of the changes in the Good Friday liturgy ordered in 1955 and 1959 is the fact that they were effected through certain pressures from the outside, and that there was the unmistakable intention of wanting to remedy an injustice or to move away from it. This innovation was meant to give origin to a thorough reflection about the position of the Jews in the liturgy, and was intended to affect the attitude of Christian people toward the Jews."[5] Henning also shows that many of the references in liturgical lessons presenting patristic texts are rather lacking in friendliness toward the Jews. "The words *Jew* and *Jewish* appear in the liturgy more frequently in an unfriendly context; seldom in a friendly manner, and then in a relative sense."[6] Concerning the total problem of Jewish guilt in the death of Christ, it might be well to cite the following passage from Henning, which gives great cause for reflection: It is not merely those who delivered Christ to Pilate, or those who received Christ in Jerusalem singing *Hosanna* that are known as *the* Jews, but it is the collective guilt of men that is being historically perpetuated. The Athenians did not have to undergo anything like it for the miscarriage of justice in Socrates, nor will the Germans have to suf-

---

[5] *Ibid.,* 132.
[6] *Ibid.,* 136.

fer similarly for the greatest mass murder of world
history."[7]

The Reproaches of Good Friday would be greatly
misconstrued if related only to the guilt and un
gratefulness of the Jews in their history and not to
our own as well.

In the lessons and the *Exultet*, the Easter Vigil
service brings a whole chapter of Old Testament
salvation-history as applicable to New Testament
salvation events: Genesis, the Red Sea, the pillar of
fire, Moses, the Promised Land; also the waters of
baptism: the flood, streams of paradise, healing of
the bitter desert waters, water out of the rock.

The Easter *Alleluia*, which is solemnly sung
during the Easter Vigil and becomes the Easter
hymn of the Christian community, also springs
from Jewish worship. Neither the translators of
the Septuagint, nor the early community, dared to
translate it. Thus it passed untranslated into the
language of worship of all peoples as a sacred heri
tage of the Old Convenant.

Then in the lessons of Easter week follows an
other great insight into Christ's work of redemption
based on the Old Testament:

Easter Monday: "To him all the prophets bear
witness, that through his name all who believe in
him may receive forgiveness of sin" (epistle). "And
beginning then with Moses and with all the proph
ets, he interpreted for them in all the Scriptures the
things referring to himself" (gospel).

Easter Tuesday: "So we now bring you the good

[7] *Ibid.*, 135.

news that God has fulfilled in us the promise made to our fathers . . ." (epistle). ". . . that all things must be fulfilled that are written in the Law of Moses and the prophets and the Psalms concerning me" (gospel).

Easter Wednesday: "The God of Abraham and the God of Isaac and the God of Jacob, the God of our fathers, has glorified his Son Jesus" (epistle). And the most important word of Peter in the same reading: "And now, brethren, I know that you acted in ignorance, as did also your rulers."

In the epistle of *Easter Thursday* we must note in particular the passage from Isaias which the minister of Candace was reading in the carriage: "He was led like a sheep to slaughter; and just as a lamb dumb before a shearer, so did he not open his mouth. . . . Then Philip opened his mouth and, beginning from Scripture, preached Jesus to him." We would also like to mention the offertory hymn of the same day for the preparation of the sacrifice (Exod. 13:5): "In the day of your celebration, said the Lord, I will bring you into a land flowing with milk and honey. Alleluia!"

In the reading of *Easter Friday*, the salvific power of the baptismal waters is praised in comparing it with the saving waters of the flood.

In the *Easter Saturday* reading from the First Letter of Peter, the prophecy of Isaias concerning the precious corner stone is interpreted as referring to Jesus Christ.

In the picture of the Good Shepherd, which reaches far back into the Old Testament (Ezech.;

Psalm 23; see also the gospel of Pentecost Tuesday), the liturgy of the Second Sunday after Easter recounts the fact of our redemption and the love of the Redeemer Jesus Christ, the core theme of the Easter celebration.

Psalm 22 has again taken a prominent position in the psalmody of present-day Christian communities.

Pentecost, the "Fiftieth Day," was likewise a Jewish feast—the harvest feast and the anniversary of receiving the law at Mount Sinai. "When the days of Pentecost were drawing to a close . . ." (Acts, 2:1–11) refers to a predestined feast. Now the Church harvests the blessings of salvation through the permeation of the spirit of Jesus. The week of Pentecost is a reliving of Easter Week, and in a similar way brings with it a plethora of references to the Old Testament. Moses' laws regarding the celebration of the Jewish Pentecost can be found in the third lesson on Ember Saturday in summer.

The liturgy of *Corpus Christi* illustrates once more the link between the Eucharistic feast and the Jewish Passover meal, and reveals the fulfillment of the Old Testament examples in the Eucharist: "He fed them with the finest wheat, alleluia! and filled them with honey from the rock, alleluia!" "In figuris praesignatur, cum Isaac immolatur, agnus paschae deputatur, datur manna patribus" (Sequence).

In the post-Pentecost cycle, only the ninth, twelfth and seventeenth Sundays are selected as most apropos for our theme:

Ninth Sunday after Pentecost: The punishment of God for His people is also an example for all humanity. ". . . and they were written for our correction, upon whom the final age of the world has come." Hardness of heart, sin and ungratefulness of old Israel may as well be the lot of those chosen and called for the New Covenant. The history of the Church unto our days testifies to the justification of the warnings and admonishments of St. Paul. Christianity has no reason whatsoever to be condescending toward the Jews. The gospel tells how Jesus wept over His city of Jerusalem. In spite of the guilt of the Jews for which He proclaimed the judgment, there always remains His love for this people.

Twelfth Sunday after Pentecost: In the reading, the New Law is compared to the Old Law. "Now if the ministration of death, which was engraved in letters upon stone, was inaugurated in such glory that the children of Israel could not look steadfastly upon the face of Moses on account of the transient glory that shone upon it, should not the ministration of the spirit be still more glorious? For if there is glory in the ministration that condemned, much more does the ministration that justifies abound in the glory" (epistle). In spite of the overwhelming glory of the New Testament, the Old Testament too remains glorious. Christ is the New Moses who truly unites us with God through His prayers and His sacrifice. The gospel describes the New Testament of Christ as the longing of the prophets and kings. In the gospel of the *Seventeenth*

Sunday after Pentecost, Jesus is designated not only as "son of David," but also "David's Lord."

Again and again, in the Sundays after Pentecost, we meet the Jewish Pharisee with whom Christ is at variance. Our Lord's accusation of the Pharisees has caused the Christian consciouness to transfer this accusation to the Jews as a group in general, and in turn caused the condemnation of that whole people. It would be wise to speak truthfully about the Pharisees in sermons as well as in the classroom, about the positive and the negative side of this religious trend in Judaism. There are many occasions to do so. This might serve as a point of departure for a thematic discussion of Israel.[8] (Self righteousness, hypocrisy, formalism, isolationism and particularism are dangers for the "righteous" of all times.) The message of the gospel is always directed to us, the Church.

The Christmas Cycle

The renewal of the Easter celebration has given cause to a thorough literary treatment of the theology and pastoral care during Lent and Easter time, for it is obvious that much ground is yet to be gained in the spiritual development of the faithful in so far as the liturgical piety of our people is just developing in regard to the Easter mystery. In general, people rank Christmas above Easter, but there can be no question of a polarity in the Church year.

[8] See H. Haag, *Biblical Lexicon,* 1329 f., and the article "Die Schriftgelehrten und die Pharisäer," in J. Schmid, *Das Evangelium nach Markus* (Ratisbon 3, 1954).

It is thus important to stress the unity of the Church year. Although Lent and Advent provide readings from Isaias, it remains that the present situation in the liturgy of the Christmas cycle, especially that of Advent, leaves much to be desired in the areas of preaching and teaching. Consequently, liturgical instruction can make a valuable contribution. For this particular season, above all, it is so vital to counteract the inevitable distractions of pre-Christmas preparations.

Advent as a period of merely waiting and getting ready has become meaningless, and therefore ought to be presented as a time for a sincere anticipation of the Lord's coming.

Perhaps it seems as if these prefatory remarks might be digressing from the theme. But actually they do lead to numerous texts of the Old Testament that tie in with this festive time during which an expectancy of the promise of salvation is being expressed. Its fulfillment begins with Christ, but is not yet accomplished.

The hopes and expectations of the Christian are always directed toward the future, which is already present in the mystery. John, the one who prepares the path and is the precursor, is the Elija of the New Testament (Matt. 7:12), the "friend of the bridegroom," who is leading the bride, the Messianic people, into the arms of the bridegroom.

Isaias is the herald of both the birth of the Lord as well as the eschatological events. It would indeed be a thankful task to put together all the passages from Isaias which occur in the liturgy of Advent, Christmas and the Epiphany. Added to such a worthwhile task would be the interpretation of the psalms in the hymns of this season as expression of our longing for redemption. Again and again Christians should call to mind the fact that Israel too was once expecting the Messiah, even if they did not recognize His arrival in the flesh.

Some of the important liturgical texts of that time will be stressed here. In the epistle of the Second Sunday in Advent, St. Paul remarks that all the books of the Old Testament were also written for Christian lore and instruction. "Whatever things have been written, have been written for our instruction, that through the patience of the consolation afforded by the Scriptures we may have hope." He even says of Christ: "Jesus Christ has been a minister of the circumcision in order to show God's fidelity in confirming the promises made to our fathers." Even the calling of the Gentiles is the fulfillment of prophecies from the Old Testament, as St. Paul proves. With this the universal character of the promise is stated and the Church of "Jews and Gentiles" prefigured. Compare also the lesson of Ember Wednesday: ". . . for the laws shall come forth from Sion, and the word of the Lord from Jerusalem. . . . Oh, House of Jacob, come, and let us walk in the light of the Lord our God." The gospel of that Ember Wednesday, the epistle of the Christmas Vigil and the gospel of the first Christmas Mass mention the origin of Jesus in the flesh from the people of Israel, from the

House of David. The epistle of the third Mass on Christmas Day states again that it is the same God who once spoke to us through the prophets, but does so now through His Son.

The Advent hymns too, so joyfully sung by the community, also lend themselves very well to liturgical interpretation. At no other time of the Church year does the Old Testament speak out in so many various songs as it does in the Advent cycle. For most of them, the Church borrows from the expectation and prayers of Israel. Christianity is found again in the words: Israel, Jerusalem, Sion. "Awake, you city of Jerusalem! Sion, hear the angels sing! Rejoice, Oh Israel!" These Old Testament themes can be found in the liturgical texts of the Second Sunday of Advent and elsewhere.

The *O-Antiphons* literally vibrate with the Messianic expectation of the Old Testament. How fitting to recall that hymns like "Oh Come, Oh Come Emmanuel" were banned as Jewish songs during the time of the Nazi regime and frequently suppressed in schools! This indicates clearly how unaware even the Christians were of their ties with Israel. The Jews and Israel were seen purely as a people and in no way in the light of faith. Nothing has remained of the "chosen people of God"—which they still were in St. Paul's letter to the Romans—except the "bad Jews" as the murderers of Christ.

In summary, we have shown through the liturgical year the close interlocking of the Old with the New Testament in the liturgy. Whoever witnesses

Christ and His Church cannot overlook the Jewish heritage in the liturgy as the most accurate self-representation of the Church.

4. Other Connections Between Church and Synagogue.

Sabbath—Sunday

Even though the Christian Sunday has replaced the Jewish *Sabbath,* the seven-day week is a carry-over from the Old Testament. There is no denying of the many traces remaining in the sabbath legislation of the new Lord's day, which has taken its name and its content from the resurrection of Christ (Exod. 20:8–11). It is true that the Christian Sunday is not merely a postponed sabbath—a fact not yet sufficiently known by Church people—but a celebration of the Old Testament week with its one day consecrated to the Lord, which is still the well-recognized basis for our own order of the week days.

The sabbath rest, however, has been transferred to Sunday. Even the Eucharist, the very heart of the Sunday, manifests considerable evidence of the Old Testament worship. The similarity between the worship of the Word with the worship of the Synagogue is sufficiently well known. The relationship of the Eucharistic meal to the paschal meal has been mentioned before. The solemn prayer of giving thanks, highlighting the Mass celebration, originates in the thanksgiving prayer of the worship meal, as well as the meal in the home of an-

cient Israel. The references to the types of Old
Testament sacrifices, Abel, Abraham and Melchisedech, are to be found in the prayers of the canon
of the Mass.

Prayers and Songs

The prayers and songs from the Old Testament
have been retained as the basic elements of Christian prayer. Let us mention only the *Sanctus* of the
Mass (Isa. 6:3), the *Benedictus* (Ps. 117:26), and the
Agnus Dei (Isa. 53:7; Jer. 11:19). The psalms, too,
are prayers and songs from the Old Testament.
The refreshing restoration of psalmody, that is,
the prayer life of the Jews, in the worship service
of today's Christian communities is like a bridge
reaching out to the Jewish people of this time. The
distribution of Martin Buber's reading of prayers
and psalms on recordings by Christian firms can
be hailed as a welcome sign of mutual understanding. The history of the Jews, that is, the history of
God with His chosen people, which is the recurrent
theme of the psalms, has become for the Christian
Church the sign of redemption, that is, the type for
the New Testament history of God with men.

The familiar greeting in the Mass, *Dominus Vo-
biscum,* stems from the Old Testament (Judg. 6:12;
Ruth 2:4); the Hebrew *Amen* should be mentioned, and even such New Testament prayers as
the *Our Father,* the *Gloria,* and the *Magnificat*
are reminiscent in form and content of Old Testament models.

Figures and Saints of the Old Testament

In spite of the great number of holy men and women in Christian history, it would not do to slight the great figures of Jewish history such as the patriarchs and prophets, judges, kings, Machabees, Esther and Judith. We encounter them again and again in the liturgical texts. The *Commendatio Animae*, the litany for the dying, makes special mention of "holy Abel" and "holy Abraham," and "all holy patriarchs and prophets." The latter are also cited in the All Saints litany. And finally, how few will keep in mind that the Apostles, so often mentioned in the liturgy, were all from the same race as the Jews?

5. Conclusion and Summary.

In the preceding essay the liturgy of the Church has been studied from the specific viewpoint of the Jews, or rather, of Jewish elements in the liturgy of the Church. It is beyond the scope of this essay, however, to examine exhaustively the connections between the Old and the New Testaments in the actual liturgical celebrations of the Church, although certain pertinent cases were featured to better illustrate the great importance of liturgical instruction.

The relationships to the Old Testament are very clear and may be detected in a multitude of examples from all liturgical books of the Church. Whoever lives with the Church—which is the aim of liturgical instruction—will foster an attitude, firmly rooted in faith, toward the Jewish people of old and the present-day Jews. The many atrocities which

were committed by this people, as cited in the
Bible, only show how much the Jews are in
need of redemption. Furthermore, their longing for
redemption sets the pace for us as well.

It is true, a new era begins with Christ. The law,
the worship, the salvific signs, the sacrifice and
much more have been renewed. But all of this has
been foretold in the Old Testament scriptures in
words and in signs. Christ does not break with the
past, which is also revelation, nor with the people
from which He comes. The rejection of Christ by
members of His chosen people is not a singular
case, but can be traced all through Christian history. Again and again the light is moved from its
place, the last become the first, the first the last,
as in the case of Esau and Jacob and the two sons
in the parable of the prodigal son.

. Consequences of Liturgical Instruction.

There is no denying that the treatment of the
theme "The Jews in Christian Religious Instruction" is unexplored territory. We must realize with
some misgiving that this topic has scarcely interested us, though we all still feel and bear the burden of the recent past. But we have only to recall
how much Christianity itself was the target of persecution, together with Judaism, and how the Christian faith was typed as a "Jewish religion." Behind
this we can discern the reality in the connection between the Old and the New Testaments. Whoever
would deny this line between the two would deny

Christ. Even silence cannot be tolerated in place
of the truth.

We might be told by some who teach that instruction today has to limit itself to a few central
themes, and that in the face of all the newness and
greatness that came with Christ and His work, we
should refrain from reaching back into the "Old,"
into a dead past. This attitude is not rare with catechists. We readily admit that it takes some effort to
teach the prophets and the psalms, or to enter into
the spirit of the Old Testament in general. But, in
principle, it cannot be denied that the Old Testament, too, holds a share in the message of the
Church. The greater the increasing lack of faith
today, the more must we center the Christian proclamation and instruction on the whole content of
Revelation. More and more the "sources" are now
being probed, that is, the Bible and the liturgy,
which work is one of the most encouraging signs in
the Church today. Many of the externals can be left
out of Christian instruction to give full vent to the
overall content of the message of salvation. Then
too, how incomprehensible the liturgy would be
were it not for a fuller knowledge and explanation of
the Old Testament texts, even though they are outmoded! With regard to the duty of retribution concerning the Jews, every opportunity should be
seized to speak of them, especially in the area o.
liturgical instruction, which lends itself so well to
this goal. There would be only a short step from
truth to love, from faith to the act.

7. Some Important Points in the Liturgical Instruction about the Jews.

Let us hastily hint at some of the central points and possibilities, and sum them up for liturgical instruction:

(1) Lent with its readings from the Old Testament;

(2) Holy Week;

(3) Advent with the figures of the prophets from Isaias and the Baptist; the content of Advent songs;

(4) the eschatological expectation of the Messiah (in connection with the liturgy of the last Sunday in the liturgical year and the Advent Sundays);

(5) Old Testament examples for the Sacraments of Baptism and the Eucharist;

(6) the origin of Christian feasts in the Old Testament;

(7) Old Testament prayers used in the celebration of the Mass;

(8) introduction of the psalms;

(9) salvation concern for Jews as well as Christians; also prayers for the Jews.

8. Examples for Liturgical Instruction about the Jews.

We would like to add three sketches for catechetical instruction:

(1) *The "Holy Land"*

(a) Point of departure: the many trips to the Holy Land in our day, including the unprecedented pilgrimage of Pope Paul VI in 1964. It is a profitable experience to visit Israel. Journeys give occasion for meeting people as well as furnish insights into the political, economic and social life of the Jews in the national Jewish home (Jordan and Israel). Faithful Christians make pilgrimages to the homeland of Jesus Christ—to Bethlehem, Nazareth, the Sea of Galilee, Cana, the Well of Jacob, Jordan, Jerusalem, Emmaus, Bethany, and Mount of Olives.

(b) Where do we confront these holy places in the study of the feasts in the liturgical year? Here the holy city of Jerusalem fits specially well: the pilgrimages, the temple, the passion, and so forth; the Second Sunday of Advent, the Fourth Sunday of Lent, the first Christian community there, and others.

(c) The objective is to emphasize the relationship of Christians to the country and the home of the Jews. It is not only the homeland of the Jews but also the "Holy Land" of Christians. "Take off your shoes, because the soil you are treading on is Holy Land."

(2) *The Prayers for the Jews on Good Friday*

(a) Good Friday with the Passion and its prayers for the Jews can be the starting point for a treatment of the "Jewish question."

(b) Good Friday recalls the sacrificial death of Christ (as in the readings, the Passion, and the veneration of the cross).

(c) During rogation-days, the Church prays for the blessings of salvation which come from the cross, for all her members and for the whole world. Here the "prayers for the Jews" should be inserted and read out loud.

(d) No human being is excluded from the mercy of Christ. He forgives Peter, Judas, and His enemies. He weeps over Jerusalem. With the love of Christ the Church prays for the Jews. This supplication should be explained and the prayers recited.

(e) In the homework-assignments, ask that prayers for the Jews be composed. In these prayers we should not only request that the Jewish people recognize Christ and His salvation of Israel according to God's promise (see Rom. 11), but also that we Christians recognize in Israel God's first chosen people, our older brethren, and learn to love that people. Compare the pastoral letter of the German bishops concerning the Eichmann Process of May 30, 1961, and the added prayers for the slain Jews and their persecutors.

(3) *The Psalms*

If the community is to really participate in the liturgical celebration, they cannot be ignorant of the psalms. Psalmody, however, demands an interpretation of the psalms. Such instruction is recommended especially in those communities where the singing of psalms is now introduced and will become a habit. The many new editions of antiphonal psalm-arrangements and their assimilation into the newer diocesan hymnals are a further expression of recognizing and needing the liturgical renewal in our times. Such singing encourages the community to participate actively in the liturgical ceremonies of the Church year.

(a) Where do we find the psalms? Diocesan hymnals, psalms in Mass texts, lauds for Easter (Ps. 129), the Asperges before a high Mass, devotions before confession (Ps. 50), and other office prayers.

(b) What are the psalms? The Psalter is a book of Holy Scripture which contains a collection of 150 prayers and songs of the people of Israel. The psalms have come down to us from times that reach back about three thousand years.

(c) In what way are the psalms used? Israel prayed the psalms during the services in the temple and the synagogue. The Church has appropriated them for her liturgy. The example of the Lord at the Last Supper: "And so they sang a hymn" (Matt. 26:30). St. Paul exhorts his people to sing psalms (Eph. 5:19; Col. 3:16). The Church has embellished her services with psalms and psalmody. Here one can mention the Mass propers and explain their antiphonal character: the antiphons for the Introit, the Offertory, and others. This comes alive in a special way during the new liturgy of Good Friday. For the celebration of the Last Supper on Holy Thursday there are four psalms utilized as communion songs.

(d) It is important to follow through from a general introduction to the explanation of some of the better known psalms and try to give them a

Christian orientation with the help of typological exegeses. From Christ a new light permeates the prayers of the time before His coming. In the psalms we praise not only the old, but also the new salvation deeds of God, accomplished in Christ.

PRAYERS FOR ISRAEL

Let us pray for the people of Israel, that God our Lord may lead them to salvation through the full recognition of the truth. Almighty and merciful Lord, God of Abraham, Isaac and Jacob, Father of our Lord Jesus Christ, You who have wrought the salvation of the world through the life and death of Your Son in the people of Israel, we beseech you:

Turn Your merciful face toward Your chosen people of the Old Testament and be merciful unto them, *graciously hear us, Oh Lord.*

Send the Holy Spirit to all the members of this people so that they may recognize You and Him whom You have sent, *graciously hear us, Oh Lord.*

Kindle in them the fire of faith so they may accept the message of Your Son, *graciously hear us, Oh Lord.*

Give unto them a holy unrest with which to seek Your will, *graciously hear us, Oh Lord.*

May the anguish suffered by this people become their way of salvation, *graciously hear us, Oh Lord.*

May those of us who by commission or omission have been found guilty toward Your people, be led to recognition of our guilt and to atonement, *graciously hear us, Oh Lord.*

Teach us to follow the example of Your Son an
to esteem and cherish the members of Israe
graciously hear us, Oh Lord.

We beseech you also that in the day of th
Second Coming of Your Son all faithful of the Ol
and New Testaments be saved and accepted int
the eternal kingdom of Your glory, *graciously hea
us, Oh Lord.*

For You, Oh Lord, are a true merciful God; You
promises and prophecies are irrevocable.

BIBLIOGRAPHY

L. Bopp, "Die religiöse Güterwelt des Alten Gotte
volkes in der Liturgie und Verkündigung de
Kirche," in *Beiträge zur christlichen Betrach
ung der Judenfrage,* ed. G. Luckner (Freibur
i. Br., 1951).

J. Hennig, "Zur Stellung der Juden in der Liturgie
Liturgisches Jahrbuch (1960), Vol. 3.

OUR BIBLE INSTRUCTION
AND JUDAISM

Adolf Exeler

he Problem.

Since almost six million Jews were murdered
der the tyranny of National Socialism, the ques-
n has often been raised—and frequently it was
ore than a question—whether Christian religious
struction could have possibly fostered the hostile
titude toward the Jews and whether it is still con-
uing to do so. Jules Isaac raised the accusation
ainst Christianity that since the time of Constan-
e it has actively been engaged in teaching "how
despise the Jews." Even the mere possibility
at there might have been a connection between
e persecution of Jews under Hitler and Chris-
n religious instruction forces us to examine what
say about the Jews in catechetics.

Bible instruction particularly cannot avoid speak-
g about the Jews. The description which we give
our students when we talk about the Jews who
ed at the time of Jesus Christ will considerably
fluence their image of the present-day Jews. It
es make a great difference if we arouse respect
d sympathy for God's chosen people—the people
Abraham, of Mary, of Jesus and His first disci-
es—or if we initiate disdain, feelings of antipa-

thy, or even a gloomy hostility toward a "stubborn treacherous, deicidal and reprobate" people.

In view of such an almost inescapable alterna tive that our Bible instruction has to face, we ar concerned with two questions:

(1) When and where does Bible instruction len itself to the danger of creating a wrong attitude i our students vis-à-vis the Jews?

(2) Where does Bible instruction offer the po sibility to create an unbiased attitude toward th Jewish people?

I. The Dangerous Passages in Bible Instructio

A. Distinction between the New and Old Testaments.

In order to demonstrate the immeasurable valu of the New Testament revelation of salvation w are tempted to overemphasize the distinction be tween the Old and New Testaments, which ofte results in a misrepresentation of the Old Test ment. By way of generalizations, the followin contrasts are likely to be made during instructio for instance, in a treatment of the Sermon on th Mount: the legislation of the Old Testament based on fear, but the legislation of the New Test ment is based on love; the Old Testament is dom nated by an external superficial interpretation of th laws strictly adhering to the letter, but the Ne Testament is distinguished by an interior associa tion and inner resemblance with the Lord.

In view of such an obviously broad and coars

eneralization we must necessarily emphasize the
herent connections between the two Testaments.
or example, in the Sermon on the Mount, Christ
ontinues to expound God's abstract demands—
ose meant for inner penetration—which are found
the prophecies. Jesus does not repudiate the leg-
lation of the Old Testament, but brings it to frui-
on.

. *Representation of the Jews at the time of Jesus Christ.*

On the basis of thorough research we know that
hristendom is derived not from a degenerative
it a religiously prolific Judaism. This is revealed
the wealth of Jewish literature at that time, the
sistance of Jews against Gentilism, the radiating
ower of Jewish piety over the Gentile world in
oselytism, and so forth. We are also aware of the
arked differences among the Jewish people at
at time.

First of all, we have to distinguish between the
aders—most of whom rejected Jesus—and the
rious groups amongst the people. Apart from
e Pharisees and the Sadducees there were the
eaceful in the land," who hoped for a religious
essiah, one who would deliver the Jewish people
om their guilt, guide them to conversion and re-
entance, and thus establish the kingdom of God.
In spite of these facts Bible instruction readily
nds to make use of generalizations. A mere glance
the commentaries used in Bible instruction re-
als the tendency to describe Judaism in the dark-

est possible background as a most effective co
trast for the radiant figure of Jesus. For the sake
accentuating Jesus, the temptation is to attribu
all kinds of basic evils to the "Jews," as if the enti
people had been dominated by a mere earthly e
pectation of the Messiah; as if most Jews had bee
superficial formalists or malevolent hypocrites;
if they had maliciously distorted Christ's word
as if "the Jews" had all been generally stubborn
their self-complacency.

Inadmissable generalizations of this nature cou
easily produce, in students, an unfriendly attitu
toward all Jews of the present; therefore such a
plications should be carefully avoided.

C. Representation of the Jews on the occasi
of Christ's passion.

In a description of the bitter sufferings of Jes
the danger of a black-and-white presentation
particularly inherent. It is at this point that one
most likely tempted to ascribe emotional facto
to the entire Jewish race: "evil Jews," "cruel Jews
In one of the recent commentaries, the followin
passage has been found:". . . but the Jews did n
feel compassion. Violent hate consumed them
view of the suffering of our Savior. Diabolical j
blinded their eyes. Soon they will have fulfilled th
dreadful desire." "The sun did not shine any mo
and it grieved. The Jews, however, remained har
ened; they encouraged and goaded one another
their hate of Christ and remained obdurate."

In this context some catechists will tell the le
end of Ahasver, the eternal Jew. Jesus wanted

est on the stairs of his house. Ahasver cursed Jesus and sent Him away. As the eternal Jew, he is now wandering about to the end of the world; he cannot find peace and shelter, and he cannot die. This legend can easily result in the students' identifying Ahasver with the entire Jewish people.

The figure of Barabbas, especially, can be the cause of generalizing black-and-white representation. It is only natural to describe Barabbas simply as a criminal and murderer: on the one hand, the evil murderer; on the other hand, the benevolent and compassionate Savior. The impression is immediately created that the Jews' choice of Barabbas had been determined by blind hate alone. It would correspond to the truth only if this event were described as follows: The crowd of Jews before Pilate believed that they were abandoned by Jesus in their worldy expectation of a Messiah. Thus they preferred the release of a resistance-fighter who could at least be expected to fulfill their political hopes.

In some commentaries, "the Jews" are termed "deicides." However, we must state clearly that the Jews are not to be called deicides, for they did not recognize Christ's divinity; and Jesus did condone their lack of recognition (Matt. 23:34). St. Peter says: "And now, brethren, I know that you did it through ignorance, as *did* also your rulers" (Acts 3:17).

If this holds true for the Jews of that time, then we are certainly not entitled to refer to the Jewish people as a people of deicides.

The cry "Let him be crucified!" (Matt. 27:22, 23)

is frequently understood as the final separation of the Jews from their Redeemer. Often the assumption is maintained that with this demand the Jews had lost their privilege of being God's chosen people and had sacrificed their title to the fulfillment of the promises. In chapter eleven of the Epistle to the Romans, St. Paul shows that this interpretation is wrong.

Another outburst of the crowd, even more distorted in its interpretation than the cry for crucifixion, is: "His blood be upon us and upon our children" (Matt. 27:25). In this context, we frequently refer to divine justice as having responded to the cry in a dreadful way: in the destruction of Jerusalem and in all subsequent persecutions of the Jews up to our day. Such misconstruction provides a serious undertone to the persecution of the Jews as if the persecutors could in any way rightfully consider themselves executors of divine justice:

What is to be said about this interpretation? Up to the fourth century the cry of the crowd in Jerusalem "His blood be upon us and upon our children" had not been construed to mean hostility toward Jews. Later, however, it often served as an argument in the fight against the Jews. From the standpoint of theology, this is a serious mistake. The blood of Christ does not cry for revenge as did that of Abel. Christ's blood was shed in order to redeem us. His sacrifice means condonation and reconciliation. When, however, Christ's blood is equalized with Abel's blood, the Jews necessarily assume the role of Cain; and then it can readily be maintained hat the Jews, like Cain, are unstable and fickle.

Whoever derives from this cry the right to hos-
ility toward the Jews shows that he does not under-
tand Christ and His gospel. Christ sent His apostles
irst to the Jews. Just as Pilate cannot be relieved
rom his guilt by washing his hands before the
yes of all, so the individual Jew or the entire Jew-
sh people cannot be held responsible for that sac-
ilegious cry.

Many commentaries for Bible instruction un-
ustly mention the reprobation of the Jewish peo-
le as the consequence of Christ's conviction. No
assage in the New Testament allows for the as-
umption that the Jewish people would have to
ear the burden of a curse, of a final rejection, or
ven of a mysterious retaliation. St. Paul vigor-
usly decries the thought that God had rejected
lis people forever. "I say then: Hath God cast
way his people? God forbid. . . .God hath not cast
way his people, which he foreknew" (Rom 11:1, 2).
n the subsequent verses, however, St. Paul does
ention a "rejection" of the Jewish people: "For
the loss of them be the reconciliation of the
orld, what shall the receiving of them be, but life
om the dead?" (Rom 11:15). Is there not a con-
adiction between the two passages? Even the
ollocation of "loss" and "receiving" reveals that
t. Paul does not have in mind a final punishment.
is true, the greater part of the people had hard-
ned their hearts against Christ's message and ac-
ordingly had been initially rejected by God. But,
s it happened in the time of Elias, the rest was

converted to God. It is important to make a prope
exegesis of the concept of "rest." One has to keer
in mind that St. Paul took this term from the Old
Testament, and that he did not, of course, thinl
in terms of modern individualistic categories. I
this is not entirely clear, one might be tempted to
construe the eleventh chapter in Romans thus: tha
the people of Israel had been rejected by God or
account of their repudiation of Christ; yet individ
ual Jews would nevertheless be able to obtain sal
vation. Such a construction is in complete contras
to St. Paul's clearly formulated statement. Th
point in question is not the Lord's relation to indi
viduals, but His relation to His people.[1]

II. Points of Departure for a Faithful Instruction about the Jews.

The question of a faithful orientation about th
Jews will be only of minor importance in Bible in
struction; it is nevertheless a task which shoul
not be taken too lightly because it is significan

A. General discussion.

The Christian appreciation of the Old Testamer
constitutes an important point of departure in ou
endeavor. Because it is the word of God, this co
lection of scriptures is highly revered as a Hol

---

[1] A. Nygren, Der Römerbrief (Gottingen, 1951), 28
The people as a people—according to St. Paul—continue t
exist in the "rest." It is represented by the "rest" that ha
turned to Christ in the hope that finally the entire peop
will be converted to God (cf. Rom. 11: 11–15).

Book by the Jews and Christians alike. The God of the Christians is also the God of the Jews. The God of Abraham, Isaac and Jacob is also worshiped by Christians. Both Jews and Christians await the kingdom of God. What separates Jews from Christians is the Christian belief in Jesus of Nazareth as the Messiah and as the Son of God, through whom the kingdom will be completed on His return. This difference is a decisive one; nevertheless, it does not destroy the fact that Jews and Christians have much in common.

B. *Individual points of departure.*

In the following we deliberately confine ourselves to those passages which are commonly taught in Bible instruction for children.

1. *Gen. 15:16, God's covenant with Abraham:* Abraham is the father of all who believe in the living God (Gal. 3). He is worshiped by both Christians and Jews (and Muslims). He is our common father. Abraham's faith is common to Jews and Christians—not only contentwise, as the belief in one God, but also formally, as unconditional surrender to His plans. Like Abraham, we are all still on the way to final salvation. His way to salvation through faith is also our way to salvation. We pray that this common point of departure may lead to the common climax: to the belief in Jesus Christ, the offspring of Abraham (Gal. 3:16).

2. *Exod. 12:13, The Exodus:* The Jews celebrated the Passover in commemoration of the exodus from Egypt. The Christian liturgy has adopted the same

event, however, with modifications (cf. the *Exultet*
and the second reading of the Easter-Vigil liturgy).
We pray that all Jewish people may recognize
Christ as our real paschal lamb and may profess
Him through faith and baptism.

3. *Deut. 5:* The Ten Commandments are holy to
Christians and Jews. The two tables can be encountered in Christian churches as well as in Jewish
synagogues. In Psalm 18 and others, Jews and
Christians thank God for this present of His love.

4. *The Psalms are the prayer-book for Jews and
Christians:* Both use many passages in the same
sense; however, many others in a different interpretation. We pray that God may guide the entire
Jewish people to the complete cognizance of His
words.

5. *Jer. 9:11:* The prophets proclaim the re-estab-
lishment of the kingdom of God by an offspring of
David. The Jews still await the first arrival of the
promised Messiah. Nevertheless, the interpretation
of the prophecies is not radically at variance among
Jews and Christians: the prophets do not only
speak of the first arrival of the Messiah, but, at
least to the same extent, of the final completion of
the kingdom of God; in this respect our yearning
resembles very much that of the Jews. It is for
this reason that Bible instruction must not only
emphasize the Messianic character of the prophecies, but must also point to the eschatological relations. We thank God because He has already
fulfilled many of His promises in His son. We pray
that He would induce the entire Jewish race to

recognize Jesus Christ as the real promised Messiah. We also pray that God may complete His kingdom soon.

Moreover, our religious instruction will have to emphasize that the prime and basic mission of the prophets is not to prophesy; in fact, there are prophets who never prophesied. Their essential task was to call back to the true God a recurringly apostate and recalcitrant people. This mission of the prophets also holds true for the Christians of the present.

6. *Exod. 36:37:* Not only does the Babylonian captivity have its twofold purpose of being a punishment for the stubbornness of the chosen people and of being, at the same time, a blessing for Jews and Gentiles (in the Jews the yearning for the Redeemer was strengthened: the Gentiles became acquainted with the living God and His promises), but the same also applies to the later persecutions of the Jews (cf. Amos 3:2 and Mach. 6:12–17). The worship of present-day Jews is similar to that of the time of the Babylonian captivity: no temple, no sacrifice; however, there is worship of the word in the synagogues. This passage may be illustrated by a visit to a synagogue or by a description of the present-day services in a synagogue.

7. *Esther:* Again and again there will be powerful men desiring to extinguish the Jewish people even up to our day. They will not succeed; on the contrary, they will be afflicted with God's punishment. The people of Israel are under His special protection.

8. *Books of Wisdom:* After the Babylonian captivity, the people of Israel experience an intensive development of their spiritual life. "After return from captivity God induces the people to reflect on the power of their faith. He leads them into a new religious community, as there is no possibility to re-establish Israel politically. In this way, the people cannot entertain hopes for salvation on earth. The Lord rather stimulates them to acquire the religious truths of the imminent kingdom of God, to act and live in accordance with what had been prophesied, and in this way to prepare for the arrival of the Messiah. The books of the Old Testament, which are written during this time, serve this aim. They oblige the individual to comply with the covenant with God after many sins and the recurring revolt in the past."[2]

9. *Dan. 7:2–18:* The prophecy of the "Son of man." Today we know that only after the Machabean persecution the Book of Daniel was compiled in the form we know today. At that time Israel recognized that redemption is not effected from below, but by direct interference from above by the son of man who comes from heaven. He will bring about the eternal kingdom of the Messiah and reign over it. Our presence in the eternal kingdom of God is no more determined by nationality, race or blood; the "Saints of the Supreme God" will be rulers.

10. *Matt. 23:34–39:* Christ's sorrow over Jerusalem. Jesus concludes even the most bitter com

[2] Ecker, *Catholic School Bible* (Dusseldorf, 1958), 152.

plaints with a blessing and a promise for His people: ". . . till you say: Blessed is he that comes in the name of the Lord!" At the end of time, Israel will be converted to Christ.

11. *Matt. 27:25:* "His blood be upon us!" The Lord had Christ's blood come upon the Jews and all men, not for reasons of revenge, but for condonation of sins. "Earth, seas, stars, and the world are cleansed by His blood" (Hymn *Pange Lingua* in the Good Friday Liturgy).

12. *Acts 2, Pentecost:* Apart from the proselytes the Church of Jesus Christ at the beginning consisted only of Jews. The 3,000 men who were baptized at Pentecost were Jews as were those who accepted the faith shortly afterwards.

13. *Acts 9:* After his conversion Saul is baptized. He is commanded to carry the faith not only to the Gentiles, but also to the children of Israel. The Jews are not disregarded in the missionary work.

14. *Acts 11:* The baptism of Cornelius, the centurion. The young Church at first was so intimately integrated into the Jewish religious life that the only way to Christ was believed to be through Judaism. God's special interference was needed so that the Gentiles could be recognized as members of the Church and be accepted directly with the same rights.

15. *Romans:* God's salvific plan for Jews and Gentiles. Israel still remains the chosen people, and before the end of time "all Israel should be saved" (11:11–36).

16. *Eph. 2:18–21:* Jews as well as Gentiles have

access to the Father. The privilege of the Jews is never disputed; the permission of direct access of the Gentiles is surprising (cf. Acts 15: the meeting of the Apostles at Jerusalem).

CONCLUSION

The gospel condemns every kind of hostility toward the Jews. It was Christ's will to tear down the "intervening wall" between Jews and Gentiles (Eph. 2:14). We, as catechists, face the invaluable but also responsible task to implant His spirit of reconciliation into the hearts of our children. I do not believe that our Bible instruction can be held responsible for the hatred of Jews during the National Socialist regime; such hatred of Jews certainly has its origin somewhere else. Nevertheless it can safely be assumed that Bible instruction has not constituted, but could have and should have, a counterbalance for the hatred of Jews. At least some of the guilt has accrued through negligence (This statement, however, is not meant to be a judgment of the subjective guilt of the catechist.) Our task will be to avoid through proper instruction any future hostility toward the Jews that might possibly stem from Christian motivation. We need to convey an objective impression of the chosen people and to caution the Christians against any unjust generalizations. We must avoid both narrow mindedness and exaggeration, and we are obliged to strive for truth and justice. We should not only proclaim the reconciliatory love of Jesus Christ but should live it ourselves accordingly.

THE OLD TESTAMENT, ISRAEL AND THE JEWS IN CATECHETICAL INSTRUCTION

Karlheinz Sorger

The founding of the State of Israel has its implications beyond the secular-political sphere and places the question of the Jewish people into new focus. Since there is again a state in which the Jewish people live together, the question of what our Christian beliefs have to say about this people reaches an ever-increasing actuality. Obviously, we shall turn for counsel to the book which in present-day Germany serves as the basis for catechetical instruction, namely, the Catholic catechism of the German dioceses, published in 1955,[1] called simply *The New German Catechism.*

This catechism, which is expected to form the religious consciousness of the young generation now growing up, will play an important part, for it will determine the content, major points and, not in the least, the "atmosphere" of faith for all German Catholics in the coming decades. The same can be applied to the Catholics in those countries where a translation of this new Catholic catechism exists and is utilized—the United States among

[1] See Father Démann, "Der Neue Deutsche Katechismus," *Freiburger Rundbrief* (1957–1958) 37–40, 17–20, for the complete treatment.

them.* Hence its contents are of great importance.

If the question of the Jewish people is placed in the light of faith, it cannot be answered without a biblical perspective. The Jew is a member of a people which God had chosen in a special manner and with whom He had negotiated a covenant. Consequently, the question of the Jew must be asked in reference to the meaning and significance of the Old Testament. Here we can pose three questions: (1) Where and how does this new catechism use Old Testament revelation? (2) How does this catechism see the connection between the Old and the New Testaments? (3) In what other connections does the catechism mention the Jews or Israel, and how is this presented?

1. *Old Testament Revelation in the New Catechism.*

There is only *one* history of God with men; it is the same God who acts in the Old Testament as in the New Testament, and speaks to men here as well as there. It is not true that the Old Testament revelations about God are antiquated or depreciated by the New Testament; both the Old and the New form *one* revelation for mankind. Bible history and the biblical catechism take this into account, and treat both Testaments. The young person hears in biblical instruction not only about the earthly life, death, resurrection and ascension of Christ, the mission of the Holy Spirit, and the growth and strength of the young Church, but also

* *The Living Faith* (New York, Herder and Herder, 1959).

about the creation of the world, the calling and the faith of Abraham, the exodus from Egypt, the law and covenant of Mount Sinai, the Kings and Prophets, and the expectation of the Messiah.

The catechism also bases its presentation of the Christian faith on the revelation of the Old and the New Testaments. Is this fact clear in the choice of texts and quotations from Holy Scripture?

Twenty-six of the 136 lessons begin with an illustrated text taken from the Old Testament, whereas 83 of these texts originate in the New Testament. The Old Testament illustrations are, of course, more predominant in the book's first part, "God and Our Redemption," particularly when speaking about God as our Father in heaven, the creation of the world, the fall of man, and the promise of redemption. The latter chapters of this part, as well as the entire second part of the catechism, "The Church and the Sacraments," contain no quotes at all from the Old Testament; however, the third part, "Life in Accordance with God's Commandments," contains many Old Testament quotes, as does the fourth part, "The Four Last Things." The unity of salvation history is especially clear in the lesson, "The Transformation of the Visible World." It would have been suitable enough to choose a quote from the Apocalypse, from the First Epistle to the Corinthians, or from the Second Epistle of Peter. Instead, the passage reads: "Through the prophet Isaias, God promised: 'For behold I create new heavens, and a new earth.'" The new heavens and the new earth represent the final for-

mation of creation in the glory of God; this was
foretold in the Old Testament, proclaimed again in
the New, and evisioned by John in the Apocalypse.

In addition to these passages, there are many
other Old Testament references in the form of concrete, symbolic quotes. In fact, the Old Testament
is alluded to in more than 120 places. More than
half of these references are found in the early
part of the new catechism, especially in the lesson,
"God Promised the Redemption." Old Testament
lore is very sparse in the second part, "The Church
and the Sacraments," and totally nonexistent in
the lessons about the Church. The reason for such
uneven usage is understandable in the light of the
respective subject matter: the Old Testament references are better applied to instruction about God
than about sacraments or eschatology. Nevertheless, it seems that the frequent use of Old Testament references in this book indicates the importance of the Jewish Covenant in catechetical
teaching.

The biblical references were selected especially
from the viewpoint of teaching. What does this
word or that event signify? What does this per-
sonage of the Old Testament say that applies to
the subject matter to be learned? It is necessary
to pose such questions, but they must be thought-
provoking in order to be effective. Thus the catechism seeks to develop in the young Christian his
attitudes of prayer. On the one hand, there is no
doubt that the new catechism in its over-all dimen-
sions, as well as in particular passages, is trying

to do just that;[2] on the other hand, it could have stressed more the inspiring words of the psalms, which are the official prayers of the Old Testament and, in addition, one of the main sources of the official prayers of the Church. More than half of the prayers of the Office are taken from the Psalter; and in every Mass celebration, every wedding ceremony, at funerals, blessings and consecrations, the Christian reads the psalms. Recently the newer diocesan prayer books have been making the psalms available in ever-increasing numbers.

The catechism, however, does not mention the praying of psalms in any of the three extensive sections on prayer, with the exception of a quote from St. Paul (Col. 3:16): "... teaching and admonishing one another in psalms, hymns, and spiritual canticles, singing in grace in your hearts to God." Likewise, there is no reference to the psalms in the lesson, "The Adoration of God." Moreover, in the thirteen pages of the Appendix, "The Christian Daily Life," which contains prayers for various occasions, we do not find any verse from the psalms, nor is there any mention of the psalms as a possible source of prayers. There is only this instance where the catechism recommends a specific psalm for prayer: (1) praying the song of the three young men in the fiery furnace; (2) praying Psalm 103; (3) depicting the creatures and things that are

[2] Cf. K. Tilmann "Der Methodische Gebrauch des neuen Katechismus im Unterricht" in H. Fischer, *Einführung in den neuen Katechismus* (Freiburg i.Br., 1955), 43: "Katechismus und Gebeterziehung."

named in these two prayers.

Thus catechists must strive to bring the psalms closer to the consciousness of children than the new catechism does. This can easily be done. First, a teacher might think of appropriate psalms and canticles while preparing the prayers before and after class (which for the lower and intermediate levels may take the form of *Children's Psalms* by E. Vizthum). In this regard the catechism itself offers a variety of possibilities. For example, note the questions in the lesson on prayer: "1. What prayers of praise and thanks do you know? 2. What hymns of praise and thanks do you know? 3. Name some prayers in which we ask for forgiveness of our sins. 4. Name some prayers in which we ask for favors." Further, another lesson on prayer advises: "Make up for yourself a form of morning prayer which expresses everything that you want to say to God at that time."

Hence it would be advisable to ask children to look for such prayers among the psalms in a prayerbook. They might discover for themselves that certain psalms simply cannot be classified in any of the above groups. This offers a good occasion to discuss with children other possibilities of Christian prayer, such as the prayer of longing for God (Psalm 62), the joy in Him, our confidence in Him.

Another "key" to the use of the psalms can be picked up at the end of Lesson 72: "Look for some prayers in the Bible." Finally, it might be well to review the entire psalm whenever a verse is cited under "Word of God" or in other places, and to use it in prayer. Similarly at the end of Lesson 66: "Why do the Psalms call God 'My fortress,' 'My refuge,' 'My Shield,' 'My light,' 'My rock'?" Here, too, the corresponding psalms could be traced and duly prayed. Wherever long passages from the psalms are to be found, as in the quote at the beginning of Lesson 17, at the end of 92, and within 99, the quoted material should rather be utilized as prayer and not merely become the object of the lesson.

The above suggestions are sufficient. For it truly belongs to the prayer life of a Christian, as well as to his liturgical formation, to know a series of psalms—not only to know them but also to realize from personal experience that one can easily talk to God in the words of the psalter.

Occasionally it should be pointed out during instruction that the psalms are the prayers which we have in common with the Jews. To be able to pray with another person, in the same words which both recognize as having divine origin, creates a unity which cannot be achieved in any other way. To impress this fact upon children will help considerably to create in them a loving understanding of the Jewish person.

2. *The Unity of the Two Testaments.*

The Old and the New Testaments belong together. In one as well as the other it is the same God who acts and speaks. Salvation history is *one*. How does the catechism do justice to this representation in its teaching about the Church?

As far as Holy Scripture is concerned, Lesson 51 puts the Old and the New Testaments side by side. Both Testaments together form Holy Scripture which is watched over by the Church as the Word of God and passed on to us. "Many of the things which God has revealed He willed to have written down in sacred books. . . . These writings are called Holy Scripture, or The Bible (which means 'The Books'). Because Holy Scripture was inspired by God, it has God for its author. It is 'The word of God.'

"Those parts of Holy Scripture that were written before Christ came are called the Old Testament; those parts which were written after Christ had come are called the New Testament.

"The Church preserves Holy Scripture as a very precious treasure. Under the guidance of the Holy Spirit she presents Holy Scripture to us, and explains it" (Lesson 51). In things to consider under Lessons 96 and 97, as well as in the concluding sections of both lessons, the most important books of Holy Scripture are enumerated: from the Old Testament the Five Books of Moses; the Books of Josue, Judges, Kings, Machabees, Job, the Psalms, Wisdom, Isaias, Ezechiel, Jeremias and Daniel.

There are other areas where the catechism finds connecting links between the Old and New Testaments. In Lesson 22 it says: "The prophets had promised God's kingdom, good men had lived in longing for it, the scribes and the Pharisees had talked about it. Jesus however announced it: 'Now is the time; God's kingdom is coming.'" In this lesson a central theme of the proclamation of the message of Jesus is presented in a wider context: the kingdom of God, promised in the Old Testament, longed for by good men, and discussed by the learned has arrived in the form of Christ.

Lesson 32, "Jesus Offered a Sacrifice of Infinite Worth upon the Cross," speaks of the fact that men of all time have brought sacrifice and explains the meaning of sacrifice, and then continues: "In Old Testament days such sacrifices were ordered by God Himself. The sacrifices which were made under the old covenant were brought to full measure of perfection in the sacrifice of the cross."

Redemption will likewise be the lot of the just ones of the Old Testament. Lesson 33, "Jesus Christ Went Down to the Dead," states: "The soul of Jesus went down to the souls of the good men who had died, and who were waiting for their redemption. Among these were the souls of Adam and Eve, of the patriarchs and prophets, and of John the Baptist. They had not yet gone to heaven because heaven was not open since Adam's sin. Now Jesus proclaimed that they were saved."

The same Holy Spirit who descended upon the Apostles at Pentecost was effective even in the Old Testament. "Already in the Old Testament the Holy Spirit had come upon the patriarchs and prophets. But on this day of Pentecost (Whitsunday) the fullness of what the Holy Spirit could give was poured out over the Apostles and disciples. Now what the prophet had said was fulfilled: 'I will pour my spirit on all flesh (i.e., mankind)' (Joel 2:28; Acts 2:17)." This is in Lesson 39.

The second item in "Things to Do," Lesson 46, makes a comparison between the Old and the New Testaments, and then inquires on behalf of both as to where God made His covenant, with whom and through what agent; also, what was sacrificed to seal each covenant.

Such connecting links with the Old Testament do not appear frequently. Although the catechism approaches the eschatological future with such admirable consistency, it fails to look as intently upon the salvation-historic past. This is obvious in the words which introduce the part, "The Church and the Sacraments," and in the subtitle, "How Christ Founded and Equipped the Church." "In God's eternal kingdom, men from every nation and from all ages are to be brought together before Him. God will be their king forever, and they will be His people. In order to make for Himself a people even here on earth, God, through His Son Jesus Christ, founded the Church." The Church appears in this part as the people of God of the New Testament, which moves toward the people of the eternal kingdom of God. But the text does not make clear that they, in their turn, are not the new but rather the fulfillment of the old covenant, the interim purpose of which was this long term of divine guidance.

The text of Lesson 46, however, seems to re establish the connection between the people of God of the New Testament with that of the Old. "God' people of the old alliance for the most part did not believe in Jesus, and their leaders condemned Him to death; they had broken their pact with God. But Jesus' disciples who believed in Him were weak and imperfect too; all men were tainted with sin, and were unworthy to be God's people.

"Jesus offered His life for His disciples, for His people that had been untrue to Him, and for all men, in order to set them free from sin and make them into a holy people of God. . . . God has made a new and eternal alliance with us in the blood of Jesus. He made the small band of disciples into a holy people of God by means of the Holy Spirit: this is our holy mother the Church. . . . When the old alliance (or covenant) was made, it was sealed by the sacrifice of our Lord Jesus Christ on the cross. . . . Eve, who was the mother of sinful mankind, had once been formed out of the side of Adam. The Church, mother of redeemed mankind, came from the side of the dying Savior. Jesus' death won life for her."

Israel and the Church, the sacrifices of the Old Covenant and the sacrifices of the New Testament, the "mother of the living," and the mother of redeemed mankind are all connected with each other.

Important as it is (and as anxious as we are to avoid a summary judgment about "the Jews"), even the above text seems to portray a much too simplified picture of Israel's role in salvation-history. For this people in the Old Testament was the people of God; its leaders rejected the Redeemer and thus broke the covenant. God makes a new alliance in the blood of Christ, but Israel as the people of God is substituted by the Church; in her, Jews and non-Jews stand side by side. But is not the Church also the "believing remnant" of Israel which is open to receive the people? St. Paul writes in his letter to the Romans (9:4 ff.) that they are "Israelites, to whom belongeth the adoption as of children, and the glory, and the testament, and the giving of the law, and the service of God, and the promises: Whose are the fathers, and of whom is Christ, according to the flesh, who is, over all things, God blessed for ever." Thus "God hath not cast away his people, which he foreknew" (11:2); furthermore, the Christians as "a wild olive" have been ingrafted in them from other peoples and have partaken of the root and the richness of the true olive, that is, of Israel (11:17). The catechist should strive to direct children's thoughts along that way, that is, by saying pointedly that Jesus Himself was a Jew; that the "small band of disciples" were Jews whom God through the Holy Spirit "has made into a holy people of God"; and that the Church thus grows out of Israel. Instruction in Church history, especially about the apostolic times, can be of help in giving a true picture of the relationship between Israel and the church.[3]

Teachings on the Holy Eucharist are contained in Lessons 75 to 79: "In the kingdom of our Father

[3] An exemplary textbook should be mentioned here: A Heuser, *Christus Gestern und heute. Eine Kirchengeschichte für junge Christen in Realschulen* (Düsseldorf, 1957). Even the table of contents reflects the theological scheme of the presentation.

we shall be forever united with Christ in the celebration of the heavenly marriage feast. With unbounded joy we shall sing God's praises; with heartfelt gratitude we shall ever remember the death of Christ, and we shall be completely filled with divine life. A guarantee and a foretaste of this heavenly marriage feast is the celebration of the Holy Eucharist."

Here, as well as in other places, the eschatological significance of the Eucharist is made quite clear.[4] Yet its relationship to the paschal meal of the Old Testament is never brought out in the passages which treat of the Eucharist. In the quotation introducing the text of Lesson 75, Jesus says: "I have greatly desired to eat this Passover with you before I suffer." But in the text itself no mention is made of the Passover meal; however, that meal deserves mention in relation to the Holy Eucharist. For the people commemorated their merciful salvation from the power of Egypt; the slaughtered animal signifies the blood of the lamb, which saved Israel from the avenging angel; and the ritual itself—the questions of the youngest family members about the significance of the Passover, the unleavened bread and bitter herbs, and the answers of the father of the house—stresses the memorable character of the feast. Beyond that the event is pregnant with Messianic expectation: "In this night they were redeemed and in this night they will be redeemed," are the words used in the Passover,

[4] Cf. Lesson 78: "In the Eucharistic meal we receive the bread of eternal life."

which were passed from generation to generation. And during this meal, in which the history and the expectations of the Old Testament are palpably present, and during which bread and wine are consumed, Christ instituted the holy meal of the New Testament, likewise a memorial of saving redemption and a guarantee of future glory.

Even though the catechism does not stress the significance of that meal in any of the lessons, it does make reference to it in two places—in Lesson 32: "For Christ, our Passover, has been sacrificed";[5] and in Lesson 77: "In the celebration of the Holy Eucharist the sacrifice of the cross is made present." It compares the celebration of the Eucharist with the Paschal Supper of the Old Testament. Catechesis might adopt this as a starting point to explain through the Bible and liturgical texts—especially those of the Easter Vigil—the comparison in the Eucharistic meal between the deliverance from Egypt and the redemption through Christ. Catechists should define what exactly both events have in common, thus clarifying their relationship, as well as the superiority of the New Law over the Old. There is an additional Old Testament quotation cited in Lesson 76: "For from the rising of the sun even to the going down, my name is great among the Gentiles, and in every place there is sacrifice, and there is offered to my name a clean oblation" (Mal. 1:11). A type of the sacrifice

[5] Here is meant the paschal lamb as model for Christ sacrificed on the cross. But the connection with the Eucharist is easily made.

of the Mass was prefigured in the sacrifice of Melchisedech who offered bread and wine. In addition, we find this assignment concluding Lesson 78: "Draw some symbols of the Holy Eucharist, for example, the manna, the pelican, wheat and grapes, the fish with the basket of loaves."

Father Démann says of the new German catechism that it is constantly using essential biblical concepts such as kingdom of God, covenant, people of God, but "nearly always on the plane of the New Testament, and cut off, so-to-say, from its roots in the Old Testament."[6] This analysis applies so far as the whole catechism is concerned; yet it cannot be denied that the assignments often try to establish such a connection with the "roots." Neither are examples nor explanations from the Old Testament used in Lesson 61 on baptism; in Lesson 88 on ordination of priests; in Lesson 53 on the worship of God, nor in Lessons 104 and 105 on the Sunday rest and feasts of the liturgical year. The only exception (other than Lesson 24, which will be discussed later) is to be found again in "Things to Do" (1), Lesson 63: "What do the Scripture readings in the Paschal Vigil tell us about Baptism?" It would be both interesting and rewarding to construct the whole catechesis on baptism from this point of departure: baptism is a new creation (first lesson); Christ precedes us and thus its waters deliver us from the power of our enemies (second lesson); through baptism we belong to those who rejoice "and are written in life in Jerusalem" (third

[6] Father Démann, *op. cit.*, 18.

lesson); baptism demands faithfulness to the new law of God from those who will enter the Promised Land (fourth lesson).

So far the above examples—Church, Eucharist, sacraments, worship and feasts—seem to show that the catechism fails to emphasize the whole of the Old Testament as a preparation for redemption. But there is one instruction dedicated exclusively to that theme, Lesson 21, "God Promised Redemption." Let us examine it.

In the introductory text the proto-gospel is used. Then the text tells of the prophecies about the Redeemer: "He is to be born in Bethlehem of a virgin mother, will be a prophet, priest and king (and therefore to be called the anointed one) and will die for mankind." The text ends beautifully: "Much of what God had promised under the old covenant was brought to fulfillment in Christ. Much is being fulfilled all the time in His Church. On the Last Day, everything that God has ever promised will be fulfilled." This lesson cites no less than fifteen prophecies of the Old Testament about the coming salvation and the Redeemer. Even the assignments probe once more the ancestry of the Redeemer, His mission and His works, His suffering and His kingdom. This lesson, therefore, offers a great variety of thought on the topic. In spite of this we notice a defect which manifests itself even in the heading. The Old Testament preparation for the redemption is being viewed only on the terms of God's promise. God had more than foretold redemption; He had

refigured it by examples, the "shadows of the future," and by His salvific action in Israel. As in
other passages mentioned previously, the figura-
tive types and the salvation-historic preparation of
redemption are not adequate even in Lesson 21.

Here another remark is in order: The lessons of
the catechism treat salvation history facts which lie
between the expulsion from paradise and the arrival of the Redeemer only in so far as the individual persons and events can illustrate certain qualities of God and His specific way of action. This is
particularly obvious in the many introductory well-
selected quotes from the Old Testament. But the
catechism fails to precede the arrival of the Redeemer with a summary presentation of the divine
salvific action.[7] The treatment of these events of
Old Testament history is often assumed to be the
task of Bible instruction; the catechism, however,
is the book which should contain not only the beliefs of the Church, but all the essentials of the
faith as well, in a form comprehensible to the young
person. And the main facts of the Old Testament
history of God with mankind seem to belong to the
essentials of the Christian faith. If the catechism
speaks of paradise and the fall and, rightly so, gives

[7] Naturally, it should not be denied that by the given
examples the history of the Old Testament can become
more apparent to young students. Here, however, we are
concerned not about individual events of the Old Testament,
but about truth of faith that God chose certain men and a
certain people in order to bring redemption in a particular
way to these people and through them to all humanity.

extensive coverage to the earthly life, passion and
death of Christ, it should also mention—perhaps in
the form of a summary called "God Has Chosen
a People and Prepared Redemption for It"—some
thing that would include the call of Abraham and
a people of God, the sealing of the old covenant
the law and the temple, the kings and prophets.

And here is a final analysis of the connection be
tween the Old and New Testaments and the role of
Israel. According to the words of the Epistle to the
Romans, "And so all Israel should be saved" (11:26)
Thus the Church teaches that the Jewish people will
be converted before the second coming of Christ
Though late, Israel will arrive at salvation. With
this the history of the chosen people will fulfill itself
Indeed Israel belongs within the Christian procla
mation, not only as the historical root of Christi
anity, but as an eschatological sign of God and a
guarantee of God's promise of salvation.

The catechism does not expressly mention the
final redemption of Israel. There is this passage
(Lesson 132, "What Christ Has Foretold About the
Time That Must Elapse Until the Last Day")
"Christ had prophesied that His message will be
proclaimed throughout the whole world until the
Last Day. All peoples are to hear the good tidings
of the kingdom of God before the end comes." But
there is much at stake in the final gathering-in of
the Jews, namely, that God "hath not cast away
his people, which he foreknew" (Rom. 11:2), but
will lead them to fulfillment. The catechist desiring
to treat this last act in the deeds of God with Israel

ight do well to continue from the above passage
Lesson 132.

The Jews in Other Sections
of the Catechism.

In addition to the topics already mentioned,
e catechism obviously ought to mention the Jews
hen treating the following: (1) Christ's Jewish
escent; (2) Christ's teaching the Jewish people;
3) Christ's suffering, death, and resurrection; (4)
irst proclamation of the young Church and her
orld mission; (5) Love of neighbor and prayers
f intercession for the Jews.

These areas of teaching will be explored subse-
uently to see if, and how, the catechism presents
e Jews:

(1) Even though the catechism does not specifi-
ally mention the Redeemer's Jewish descent, the
atechist will find a series of allusions that point to
his important fact. The explanatory texts in Les-
ons 27 and 28 cite Nazareth as the city where the
rchangel Gabriel visited Mary, and Bethlehem
s the place where the Three Wise Men worshiped
he Child. The prophecies in Lesson 21 foretell the
ew covenant with the house of Juda, the shoot
rom the rod of Jesse, and Bethlehem as the birth-
lace of the Messiah-king. In the lesson's assign-
nent, we find: "1. What do the prophets say about
a) the ancestry of the Redeemer; (b) about His
nission and works? 2. Which promises have already
een fulfilled?" These allusions are helpful only to
he young people who have been sufficiently indoc-

trinated in the study of the Old Testament and th
Holy Land.[8]

(2) The first people who heard the proclamatio
by Christ were the Jews. And this is not by acc
dent: Christ had first been sent "to the lost shee
of Israel." His message had first been destined fc
the Jewish people, then for others. The catechisr
merely alludes to this, for instance, in the quot:
tion found in Lesson 22: "God has visited his pec
ple" (Luke 7:16).

(3) In Christian instruction the subject matte
involving the greatest risk in anti-Jewish feeling
is the passion of Christ. A. Exeler provides alarm
ing examples taken from catechetical instructions
In contrast, however, the corresponding catechisr
text in Lesson 29 is a model of carefully differen
tiated presentation. Even the heading of the lessor
"The Son of God Was Rejected by the Leaders c
the Chosen People," rebukes the assumed judg
ment blaming "the Jews" for the passion and deat
of our Lord.[10] The text reads: "The chosen pec
ple had heard the words of Jesus and had seen th
miracles He performed, and the holy way He livec
Yet *many of them* would not listen to the messag

[8] The figures in the Bible, especially that of Jesus, mus
never stand in a vacuum. Therefore, it is essential that som
knowledge of biblical history and of the conditions an
habits of Palestine at the time of Jesus be given to th
young in a form they can understand.

[9] See his essay, "Our Bible Instruction and Judaism," i
this book.

[10] None of the texts so far mentioned a "chosen people,
which is another proof for what we have said on page 7
about the close connection with the salvation-historic pas:

hich He had come to give. Their leaders stirred
he people up against Him and condemned the Son
f God to death. Many of *His disciples* left Him too,
nd Judas, one of the twelve Apostles, betrayed
Him." Behind this manifold human guilt lurk the
owers of darkness: "It was *the devil* who led men
nto all these sins. He now saw that his power
ould be brought to an end if men were to believe
n Jesus and follow Him. Therefore he used all his
ower to see that men should reject the good news
hich Jesus brought, and should put Him to death."
hat it was the Jewish people who rejected Him is
ot decisive, but rather that they were *men in sin:*
That men should have rejected the Son of God is
deep and awful mystery. All the sinfulness and
eakness of man can be seen in this rejection. It
ows us what frightful ruin sin has worked in the
arts of men."[11] It was *sinful mankind* that re-
cted its Redeemer. Thus the quote from John
plies: "He came unto his own, and his own re-
ived him not" (John 1:11).

The men who through their own frailty rejected
hrist are the ones immediately responsible for the
assion. That is why, in the lesson's assignment,
e find a question which helps the students trace,
 themselves, the guilt of the individuals: "How
 the passion of Jesus did the weakness and sinful-
ss of men show itself: (a) among the leaders of

[11] We would have expected a clear reference in the text
at it was the sins of the whole world, that is, our sins as
ll, which caused the sufferings of Jesus. As the texts go
, this thought becomes somewhat clearer.

the people; (b) among the people; (c) in Pontiu
Pilate; (d) in Judas; (e) in Peter; (f) in the othe
Apostles?" The Jews' failure to repent is also
part of the guilt: "Jesus complained about Jerusa
lem, a city that would not do penance: 'Jerusalen
Jerusalem, thou that killest the prophets and stor
est them that are sent to thee; how often would
have gathered together thy children, as the he
gathers her chickens under her wings, and tho
wouldst not?'" (Matt. 23:37). But every sinner
likewise guilty; thus St. Paul says of the sinne
that they crucify "again to themselves the Son o
God" and make of Him a mockery (Heb. 6:6
Every one of us is guilty, too: "I shall not take m
sins lightly, for they have also added to the pai
Christ had to undergo" (Lesson 29). Once mor
this same lesson indicates that it is the sins of a
mankind that made Christ suffer: "On Good Fr
day the Church sings the Savior's song of con
plaint for the ingratitude of His people and *of a
mankind.* It begins: 'Oh my people, what have
done to you? In what have I offended you?'"
The following texts of instruction are also free o
any one-sided accusation of the Jews. They ref
to them generally as the "enemies" of Jesus (Le
son 30): "Jesus knew that His enemies would co
demn and crucify Him. . . ; He even prayed on th
cross for His enemies. Jesus gave His life out
love for us sinful men." Also Lesson 35: "The en

[12] Cf. "Jesus offered His life for His disciples, for F
people that had been untrue to Him, and for all me
(Lesson 46).

ies of Jesus could not deny His resurrection."

Of the above texts, particularly Lesson 29—im-
ued as they are with the spirit of catechesis—it
an indeed be said that they have done justice to
ie "Jews" who were so often accused of deicide.

(4) The proclamation of the Apostles and disci-
les following Pentecost was first of all directed
· their own people, but soon enough to the Gen-
les as well. We thus read in Lesson 39: "The Apos-
es and disciples were enlightened by the Holy
pirit. . . ; He gave them the right words with
hich to proclaim the message of their Lord *to both
ie Jews and the pagans.*" The basis for such mis-
onary activity of the young Church lies in the
ommandment of Christ: "Going therefore, teach
· all nations" (Math. 28:19). And this passage from
ie scriptures introduces the instruction in Lesson
?, "The Church's Mission to Preach Everywhere."
s text teaches about "one of the most important
sks of the Church," the proclamation of the good
dings. It is directed to "all creation," therefore
so, as in the beginning of the Church, to the
ws.[13] But is this specifically mentioned in the
struction? Hardly, for the text directed to those
ithin the fold of the Church reads: "There are
ill millions who are waiting to hear the joyful
ws of Christ. . . . If we love Christ, we shall do
l in our power to help *pagans* learn the truth and

[13] There are differences concerning the mission of the
ws between the times of the Apostles and the present-day.
ere is meant only the basic kinship of the Jews with the
cipients of the message.

so come to faith in Christ." According to the abov
words, the mission is directed only to pagans; ne
ther Jews nor Mohammedans are mentioned. Tha
the schema on non-Christians deals only with pa
gans is obvious, especially since the text speak
only about pagans and then gives the following st
tistics: "More than two thirds of the world are n
yet Christians. About 57 million children who com
into the world every year are not baptized." Or i
the passage on the most important mission soci
ties: "Holy Mary Mother of God, pray for us an
for all *poor pagan children*." Or in the assignmen
"1. Name some great missionaries of the pagans
To simply say *missionaries* would suffice here. It
understandable, of course, that the Jews would n
be expressly mentioned, for where in the world
there a mission for the Jews? But then, at leas
the Mohammedans are worthy of mention, becau
there are missionaries among them. At the most, w
could expect some formulation in the text whic
leaves room for Jews and Mohammedans alon
side the pagans, namely, the term "non-Chri
tians." Therefore, the catechist who is teachin
about the world mission should certainly stre
these differentiations.[14] At any rate, in talkin
about mission statistics it would be wise simply
question if all the 57 million children who will com
into the world, and will not be baptized, are pa
gans? In order to distinguish between the thr
religious groups and the respectively different mi

[14] Indications for this may be found in Tielman-Die
Der Weltweite Ruf (Munich), 286.

ions imposed upon the messengers of faith, a cate-
hist ought to ask: "What should the missionary
roclaim to the pagans? What to the Jews? And
vhat to the Mohammedans?"

(5) The first and greatest commandment of Chris-
ianity (and also of the Old Testament) is that of
ove for God and neighbor. Lesson 68 deals with
ove of neighbor. We may not exclude anyone
rom our love, even if he speaks another language,
r belongs to another race, or has another reli-
ion. These words are a clear denunciation of all
acial, political, and religious discrimination. Even
 the Jews are not singled out, they are under-
tandably included here, something that even chil-
ren can detect easily. More than likely, children
nswering the final question in this lesson, "What
eople especially need our love?" will name the
ews; this would mark a good occasion for the cat-
chist to discuss with children love for the Jewish
eople and to carefully correct, if necessary, any
vrong concepts.

Love of neighbor is also manifested through
rayer. In Lesson 72, "The Arranging of Prayer,"
nly those are mentioned who are close to us, or
vho particularly need our prayers: parents, sisters
nd brothers, benefactors, the sick and the dying,
ie pastors of the Church and the leaders of the
eoples, sinners and pagans.[15] There it would be
esirable to include the Jews, by name, as they
re in the Good Friday liturgy. This can easily be

[15] It also appears here that "non-Christians" implies the
pagans," as in Lesson 52.

done, possibly by adding a comment to the text which presently reads: "The Christian is to shut no one off from his prayers: God loves everyone and Christ died for all men."

Perhaps by this time, at the end of the third part, an analysis should be made as to how the catechism treats the Jewish question in the passages mentioned. What attitude does the catechism reveal toward the Jewish person? It seems that all in all not enough mention is made of Israel. However, whenever mention of the Jews appears, it is never given in a glibly generalizing manner, nor does the mention of Jews ever afford the slightest occasion for anti-Jewish attitudes. As far as the present catechist-writer is concerned, the reproach that our religious instruction furthers anti-Jewish attitudes is unfounded. We must continue to hope that our present catechesis is filled with the same spirit and that it will help us to comfort the Jewish persons in justice and love.

THE JEWS IN THE ROMAN
CATECHISM

Gerhard Bellinger

This chapter will attempt to analyze the question
of the Jews as the Roman catechism treats it.[1]
The actual title of this catechism, which appeared
in Rome in 1566, is *Catechismus ex decreto Concilii
Tridentini ad parochos Pii V iussu editus (Catechism Published According to the Decisions of the
Council of Trent for Parish Priests by Order of
Pius V)*. Such an analysis is of considerable importance inasmuch as that particular Roman catechism (which hereafter will be cited as *Catechismus Romanus*) has become in the past centuries
the world's authentic handbook for priests in the
field of preaching and catechesis. Furthermore,
this official Roman catechism, endorsed by the
Council of Trent itself, is characterized by such
renowned authorities in catechetics as no other catechism can claim.[2]

Let us preface our endeavor by a brief presentation of the Jewish question as it existed in the
Tridentine days, because it will help to better un-

[1] This analysis is based on the Ratisbon *Catechismus
Romanus*, 1896 edition.
[2] Cf. P. Paschini, *Il Catechismo Romano del Concilio di
Trento* (Rome, 1923), 7 ff.

derstand the testimony of the *Catechismus Romanus* and to better evaluate the peculiar nature o
this catechism against the historic background o
the times in which it was written.[3] What was th
position of the Church regarding the Jews at th
time of the Council of Trent? What was Pius \
who ordered the *Catechismus Romanus* to be wri
ten, doing toward the conversion of the Jews?

At the beginning of the sixteenth century th
popes had other preoccupations besides being cor
cerned about the mission of the Jewish people.]
was only the spread of Protestantism and the Cour
ter Reformation that roused new apostolic zeal and
in turn, affected the question of the Jewish mi:
sion.[4] Above all, the popes began to see that the
could convert the Jews through sermons especiall
slanted toward them. Thus Pope Paul IV, wh
reigned from 1555 to 1559, had sermons preache
to the Jews in the Papal State.[5]

And Paul V (1566–1572) decreed that from th
year 1568 sermons were to be preached to the Jew
on all holydays[6] and insisted, under heavy pen
alties, that these sermons be frequented by th
Jews.[7]

---

[3] See also F. X. Thalhofer, *Entwicklung des katholische
Kathechismus in Deutschland von Canisius bis Deharb*
(Freiburg i. Br., 1899) 9 ff., 37 ff., 75 ff.

[4] Cf. P. Browe, "Die Judenmission im Mittelalter und di
Päpste," *Miscellanea Historiae Pontificiae*, edited by th
faculty of Church History at the Gregorian Pontifical Un
versity, Vol. II (Rome, 1942), 39.

[5] *Ibid.*, 40.

[6] *Ibid.*

[7] *Ibid.*, 54.

What were the topics treated in these sermons?

During the High and Late Middle Ages, the objective was, on the one hand, to present "the reason for the rejection of Israel through the destruction of the Temple in Jerusalem—which was never rebuilt—and their diaspora which had now lasted well over a hundred years, and, on the other hand, to prove that Christ was the Messiah and that His Church was the successor of the Synagogue."[8] We may safely assume that such themes on the Jews as far back as the Middle Ages have to some degree influenced the themes of sermons in modern times. To our knowledge there has been no other directive for preaching to the Jews from any of the Tridentine popes.

If Jews were wanting baptism, a long time of preparation was required of them. Because of the fact that many Jewish converts of the early days had gone back to the beliefs of their fathers, the Visigoth Synod of Agde had decreed as far back as the year 506, that Jews had to remain catechumens for eight months—a time of preparation much longer than that required of pagans.[9] Paul II, pope from 1534 to 1549, had asked of them an even longer time of preparation in 1542:[10]

When the seventy-year-old head of the Synagogue in Rome became converted to the Christian faith together with his three sons and one grandson, Pope Pius V personally administered their bap-

[8] *Ibid.*, 45.
[9] *Ibid.*, 140.
[10] *Ibid.*, 149.

tism. This baptism was celebrated with great ceremonials, in the presence of many cardinals and a great throng of people, on the third day of Pentecost in 1566 in St. Peter's Cathedral.[11] "Pius V imparted his own name to Elias—this was the name of the head of the Synagogue and accepted him into the family of the Ghislieri. "He adopted the seven-year-old boy, now a noble, newly-created Christian by the name of Paul. Later he sent him, together with two of his nephews and in company of one of his camerlengos, to the Jesuit General for education in the Collegium Germanicum, and recommended him warmly. The two, he said, were his nephews, but Paul was his son."[12]

This papal gesture induced many Jews to become converted. But the converted Jews turned out to be a perpetual worry for the popes. Because of their closeness with other Jews who had remained true to the old beliefs, these new converts were in constant danger of retroversion or apostasy. In view of these risks the popes tried to separate the newly converted from the others, and even intimidated these Jewish converts by threatening heavy fines in case of apostasy.

Thus Pope Paul III in the year 1542 renewed the ordinance of the Basle Synod in regard to the Jews.[13] In 1568 Pius V forbade the converted Jews to set foot into the Roman ghetto, or to eat or drink

[11] L. Pastor, *Geschichte der Päpste,* VIII (Freiburg 1923), 248.

[12] Browe, *op. cit.* ,157.

[13] *Ibid.,* 170.

with their unconverted brethren, threatening heavy reprisals. The punishment incurred by disobeying this ordinance was a three-day period of public torture for men, and flailing for the women.[14]

The popes also provided for the further religious formation of the Jewish neophyte by instituting homes which the popes maintained. This was done by Paul III,[15] Julius III (1550–1555) and Paul IV.[16] Pius IV and Pius V designated a special monastery for those Jewish neophytes who wanted to enter an order.[17]

Pius V, under whose pontificate the *Catechismus Romanus* was first published in Rome in 1566, paid special attention to the mission of the Jews, as we have seen. But at the end, this pope, who in 1566 still had ordered bodily punishment for all those who would harm the Jews willfully,[18] had the Jews expelled within three months from all the territories of the Papal States, except the cities of Rome and Ancona. It may have been that the disappointingly low numbers of Jews who were converted to Christianity had something to do with this decree. "Whoever is found on Papal territory after the expiration of this term will lose all his property and become a slave of the Roman Church."[19] During these expulsions, cases of duress and of "direct or indirect

---

[14] K. Hoffman, *Ursprung und Anfangstätigkeit des ersten päpstlichen Missionsinstitutes* (Munster, 1923), 125.
[15] Browe, *op. cit.,* 176.
[16] *Ibid.*
[17] Hoffman, *op. cit.,* 84 ff.
[18] Pastor, *op. cit.,* 244.
[19] *Ibid.,* 246.

pressure were not entirely absent."[20] Karl Hoffman has this to say: "Though Pope Pius V was so much interested in the conversion of the Jews, by expelling them he became the first among the successors of Peter who deviated from the habitual role of protector, a role held by the popes throughout the centuries."[21]

And now let us take a good look at the *Catechismus Romanus.* This book is divided into four parts: symbols, sacraments, commandments and prayers. Consequently, our analysis will show the four parts paralleling the above.

I. *Church and Synagogue.*

As might be expected, we can find many references linking the explanation of the articles of faith treating Jesus Christ and His redemption with the people of God of the Old Testament. These articles of faith will be covered in the third part. The ninth article of faith treats of the Church: *Credo Sanctam Ecclesiam Catholicam.* After a short introduction concerning the significance of this chapter at that time (the Reformation), the definition of Church stems from the word *ecclesia.* Church means "calling." The faithful are called by way of belief. God has chosen the faithful to make of them the "people of God."[22] We note here that it is no longer the Synagogue but the Church which is the

[20] Browe, *op. cit.,* 243.

[21] Hoffman, *op. cit.,* 132.

[22] Significat autem ecclesia *evocationem* . . . qui (fideles) . . . per fidem *vocati sunt* (I, 10, 2); qui (Deus) eos, *ut populos Dei* esset, elegit (I, 10, 4).

chosen people of God. Immediately after this the great difference between Church and Synagogue is stressed. The term *ecclesia* should keep alive memories of the salvific calling and of the high aim of the Christians:

> He who wonders why that faithful people which once respected the law, was called Synagogue, that is, herded-in, will best understand it by the characteristics inherent in this calling—the recognition and possession of eternal things. As St. Augustine teaches, they were given that name because, like a herd of cattle driven together from all parts, they were looking to earthly and passing goods. And for this reason the Christian people are rightfully not called Synagogue but Church, since they disdain the things of this earth which are passing, and follow only the heavenly and eternal things.[23]

In spite of the great divergence between the faithful of the Old Testament and that of the New, a definite unity exists in the one church. Upon examining the "Catholic" quality of the Church, we read:

[23] Praeterea ex hac vocatione quis nobis finis propositus esse debeat, nimirum aeternarum rerum cognitio et possessio, is optime perspiciet, qui animadverterit, cur olim fidelis populus sub lege positus "synagoga," id est congregatio, diceretur. Nam, ut docet Sanctus Augustinus, hoc ei nomen impositum est, quia pecudum more, quibus magis congregari convenit, terrena et caduca tantum bona spectaret. Quare merito Christianus populus non synagoga, sed ecclesia dicitur: quia terrenis et mortalibus rebus contemptis coelestes et aeternas tantummodo consectatur (I, 10, 3).

All faithful who have lived from Adam to this
day and shall live as long as the world will exist,
and who profess the true belief, belong to this
Church, which is established "on the foundation
of the Apostles and the Prophets" (Eph. 2:20),
who on their part rest on the "cornerstone of
Christ" who has united the two parts in one
and proclaimed peace to the far and the near
(Eph. 2:14–17).[24]

In his letters to the Ephesians St. Paul refers to
both Jews and pagans when he speaks of "the two
parts." He also makes reference to the fact that
the Church has its origin in the Old Testament:

Since the examples of the Old Testament have
a great influence on the sentiments of the faithful and evoke memories of the most beautiful
things—reasons for which the Apostle used these
parables in the first place—the pastors should
not therefore neglect this extremely important
part of teaching. Another example is the great
city of Jerusalem,[25] whose name the scriptures
often use when speaking of the Church. Only in

[24] Praeterea omnes fideles, qui ab Adam in hunc usque
diem fuerunt, quive futuri sunt, quamdiu mundus exstabit
veram fidem profitentes ad eandem ecclesiam pertinent
quae "super fundamento Apostolorum" fundata est, "ae
Prophetarum" qui omnes, in illo "lapide angulari Christo,"
qui fecit utraque unum, et pacem iis, qui prope, et iis, qu
longe, annunciavit, constituti sunt et fundati (I, 10, 16).

[25] First the simile of the arc is used, which is often found
in *Catechismus Romanus*. We shall bypass everything tha
happens before Abraham, with whom begins the history of
the chosen people.

her was it permitted to sacrifice, because the true cult and the true victim is never to be found outside the Church, the only one which pleases God.[26]

In the chapter on "Communio Sanctorum" we read:

In her (the Church) there are different members among the various people: Jews and Gentiles, free men and slaves, rich and poor; but once initiated through baptism they form one body with Christ, of which He is the head.[27]

Both Jews and Gentiles are then called to find salvation in this Church. That the Church is the successor of the Synagogue is made especially clear in the following part on the sacraments which contains a quotation from Dionysius the Areopagite (De eccl., hier, 5, 2):

If we consider the dignity of the glorious sacrament (the Eucharist), we can compare it to the glory and fulfillment of the New Law, which pos-

[26] Sed. quoniam magnam vim habent figurae veteris Testamenti ad excitandos fidelium animos, revocandamque rerum pulcherrimarum memoriam, cuius rei potissimum causa Apostoli his usi sunt: illam quoque doctrinae partem, quae magnas utilitates habet, parochi non praetermittent ... Alia figura est magna illa civitas Hierusalem, cuius nomine Scripturae saepius sanctam ecclesiam significant. Nimirum in illa solum offerre Deo sacrificia licebat, quia in sola etiam Dei ecclesia, neque extra eam usquam, verus cultus verumque sacrificium reperitur, quod Deo placere ullo modo possit (I, 10, 19).

[27] ... in qua etsi diversa sunt membra, nempe variae nationes, Judaeorum, gentium, liberi et servi, pauperes et divites, quum tamen baptismo initiantur, unum corpus cum Christo fiunt, cuius ille caput est (I, 10, 25).

sesses that which in the Mosaic Law existed only in the form of signs and symbols. For this reason and through divine grace, Dionysius said, that our Church stands in the middle between the Synagogue and the celestial Jerusalem, and therefore partakes in both.[28]

As for explaining the word "Amen" at the end of the Our Father, we read:

This Hebrew word was so often pronounced by the Redeemer, that it pleased the Holy Spirit to retain it in the Church of God (Hebraea vox, IV, 17:4).

Concerning the twelfth article of faith and "eternal life," the *Catechismus Romanus* says:

Even though many names are used in Sacred Scripture for the heavenly bliss, such as Kingdom of God, Kingdom of Christ, Holy City, New Jerusalem, and others, we can clearly see that none is adequate to explain the elevated state (sancta civitas, nova Jerusalem, I, 13:4).

In Christ the Old Covenant has found its fulfillment.

When the celebration of the Sabbath was abolished with the death of Christ, the other Hebrew forms of culture and ceremonies simultaneously

[28] Primum enim intelligunt, quanta sit evangelicae legis perfectio, cui datum est, id re ipsa habere, quod signis tantum et figuris Mosaicae legis tempore adumbratum fuerat. Quare divinitus dictum est a Dionysio ecclesiam nostram esse inter Synagogam et supremam Hierusalem, ac propterea utriusque participem (II, 4, 32).

had lost their significance; since these ceremonies, so to speak, are shadows of the light of truth, they had to disappear as soon as the real light of truth, Christ, appeared (quo ceteri Hebraici cultus caeremoniaeque antiquandae erant, III, 4:5).

The Synagogue was only a sign (figura) of the Church, and the latter is now the one and true chosen people of God. The Church, which was founded by Jesus Christ, has become the successor of the Synagogue. But even this Church is still on its way to Jerusalem. These are the main thoughts of this chapter.

II. *The Sacraments of the Old and the New Testaments.*

The first chapter of the second part of *Catechismus Romanus* treats of the sacraments in general. It states that there were sacraments even in the old covenant (II, 3, 1.) Thus the circumcision is called a sacrament of the Old Law (II, 1, 7). However, the sacraments of the New Testament are superior to those of the Old.

Compared with the sacraments of the New Law, those signs in the Old Testament, which were instituted by God himself, have only the demonstrative and not the effective power as, "for instance, the cleansing, the unleavened bread and many others" (II, 1, 9). Now the sacraments of the Old Law are abolished "by the law and the grace of the gospel" (II, 1, 3,).

In the following chapters, which treat the sacraments individually, there are numerous references linking the Old Testament with the New.

Baptism, it states, was prefigured by God in the examples and words of the prophets (tum figuris, tum prophetarum oraculis). The passage through the Red Sea was a sign for the waters of baptism; the cleansing of Naamann the Syrian, the miraculous strength of the sheep pond and many other incidents are open to a representation of this mystery (huius mysterii symbolum).

In connection with the words of the prophets, mention is made of the waters to which Isaias invites all those who thirst; of the stream of water Ezechiel saw flowing from beneath the threshold of the temple (Ezech. 47:1); as well as of the fountain which Zacharias prophesied for the clansmen of David and the citizens of Jerusalem to rid them of guilt and defilement (Zach. 13:1, II, 2, 9,).

In order to justify infant baptism, attention is called to circumcision, which was a type of baptism (circumcisio quae figura fuit baptismi, II, 2, 32). To illustrate the efficacy of baptism by which sin is taken away, mention is again made of Naamann, the Syrian, who was so thoroughly cleansed from leprosy by washing seven times in the River Jordan, that his flesh became as fresh as that of a child (II, 2, 44).

The Holy Eucharist as a meal was prefigured in the Old Testament. In describing the institution of the Holy Eucharist the catechism says:

. . . He had eaten the paschal lamb with His disciples, so that the shadow of truth might give way to the real truth (ut figura veritati, umbra corpori cederet, II, 4, 2).

The matter of the Eucharist is wheat bread, as the example in the Old Testament teaches:

It was prescribed by the Lord that the wafers, which point to this sacrament, must be made from wheat flour (veteris Testamenti figura, II, 4:12).

According to Christ's law, the matter should be made of unleavened bread:

He himself has instituted the sacrament (primo azymorum die), since the Jews were not allowed to have any leaven in their houses (II, 4, 13).

With respect to the words of consecration we read:

The words of the New Covenant were added in order to affirm that the blood of Christ is not a symbol, as it is in the Old Testament; in the New Testament it is indeed His actual blood that is truly presented to man (Christi Domini sangiunem non figura, quemadmodum in veteri Testamento fiebat, II, 4, 23).

A vivid illustration of the fact that worthy preparation for the Eucharist is conducive—and unworthy preparation causes perdition—lies in the meaning of the thora.

Nothing of worth remained to the Jewish people, though the Lord had spared them; to the Philistines, however, who carried them off, it brought the worst plague, damage and eternal shame (II, 4:56; I Kings 5:1 ff.).

The manna which daily regenerated the strength of the body was a sign for frequent, even daily, communion (II, 4, 60).

A symbol of the fact that the Eucharist is both a sacrifice *and* a meal becomes obvious in the paschal lamb, which was always presented as a sacrifice and then consumed."[29]

That the Eucharist is also a sacrifice is shown in the perfectly unequivocal prophecy of Malachias (Mal. 1:11). This sacrifice had been prefigured both before and after the law by various forms of offering. All such prefigured offerings, it seems, are contained within that one sacrificial gift as a fulfillment of them all. The most lucid example of this is Melchisedech's sacrifice. The Redeemer Himself said He was a priest of the order of Melchisedech for all eternity, when He presented His own flesh and blood under the guise of bread and wine to the Father (II, 4, 75).

Even though the sacrifices of the Old Testament were types for the New, the latter are superior in value. If the sacrifices of the Old Testament

[29] Huius rei figuram et similitudinem in agno paschali licet animadvertere, qui ut sacrificium et sacramentum a filiis Israel offerri et comedi consueverat (II, 4, 70).

were so pleasing to the Lord that He accepted them in favor, how much more can we expect of a sacrifice in which He Himself is slaughtered and sacrificed and of whom the divine voice has twice been heard to say: "This is my beloved son in whom I have been pleased" (II, 4, 69).

The Sacrament of Penance is also seen in relation to events of the Old Testament:

When we are looking for examples in the Old Testament, there is doubtless a connection between the confession of sins and the many kinds of sacrifices brought by the priests in atonement for sin (veteris Testamenti figura, II, 5, 41).

The form of this sacrament exposes still another great difference between the Old and the New Testaments:

It is not as it was in the Old Testament, when the priests would pronounce a sick one cured of his leprosy (III Mos. 13:9). Now the priests in the Church not only have the power to make a declaration but also the power to actually absolve a penitent as a servant of God (II, 5, 16).

The unity of both Testaments is clearly reflected in the Sacrament of Holy Orders. In explaining the effect of the tonsure as a step toward ordination the catechism states:

The name of cleric comes from the fact that he now has the Lord as his lot and his heritage, as it was once in the people of Israel with those who were destined for the service of God. The Lord has denied them any part of the fields in the Promised Land because He said: "I am their lot and their heritage (IV Mos. 18, 20; II, 7, 13).

The catechism further speaks of a twofold priesthood that had existed in the Old Testament, one interiorly and the other exteriorly:

David spoke of the inner priesthood(Ps. 50:19); for the outward one, the Lord has given Moses and Aaron many directions. In addition, He had made the whole tribe of Levi into servants of the Temple, and prohibited by law that anyone from another tribe would assume such a task. Thus King Ozias was smitten with leprosy by the Lord because he assumed some priestly offices, and had to atone for his arrogant gesture (II Par. 26:19).[30]

There is a great difference between the priesthood of the Old and that of the New Testament. Even though priests at all times possessed the highest honors, those of the New Testament surpass the others by far (II, 7, 2). The people of Israel by no means lacked in power of consecration. Even though such power was superior in dignity to that of the priests of the natural law, it is by far below the dignity of priests of the evangelical law . . . for their power does not go

[30] Hoc sacerdotii discrimen in veteri etiam lege observari potest; . . . de interiori Davidem locutum esse . . . externi vero nemo ignorare potest . . . (II, 7, 24).

back to the Mosaic priesthood, but to Christ the Lord Himself (II, 7, 8).[31]

From the priests is asked a sanctity of life. "The infirmities, which according to the Old Law excluded a man from priestly service, are in a wider sense to be interpreted in the evangelical law as spiritual deficiencies" (in veteri lege—in evangelica lege, 11, 7, 31).

In the Sacrament of Matrimony a great difference is underlined between the truly sacramental matrimony and the type performed before and after the Law:

How greatly the sacrament of matrimony surpasses the nuptials before and after the Law. . . . The marriages of Gentiles lacked the supporting strength of a sacrament. The Jews kept their vows much more faithfully, and there is no doubt that their marriages bespoke a great sanctity. . . . But even so, such ceremonies were without the true character of a sacrament.[32]

The following passage treats the indissolubility of matrimony:

From all this it is clear that the marriages of the faithful greatly surpassed in perfection and no-

[31] Eadem etiam potestate populus Israeliticus non caruit; . . . superior . . . in lege naturae sacerdotes . . . inferior, quam legis evangelicas spiritualis potestas . . . (II, 7, 8).

[32] . . . matrimonii sacramentum iis matrimoniis praestet, quae ante vel post legem iniri solebant . . . eorum (Judaeorum) matrimonia maiori sanctitate . . . sed illae quoque coniunctiones vera sacramenti ratione caruerunt (II, 8, 18).

bility those unions among the Gentiles as well as those of the Jews.[33]

In that part of *Catechismus Romanus* which treats the sacraments, the connection between the Old and the New Testaments is stressed, as we have seen, even though the latter is far superior to the former in strength. There is, however, no reference to the Old Testament in the case of the Sacrament of Confirmation or the Sacrament of the Sick.

III. *The Jews as God's chosen people of the Old Testament.*

At the beginning of the third part of *Catechismus Romanus,* which covers the commandments, the history of the chosen people is observed much more closely because a great deal of "what seems to be valid only for the Jews applies as well to Christians, if one considers the inner plan of salvation."[34]

In another place it states that "though the law was given by God to the Jews, God wanted all people to be subject to him. . . . Therefore it is highly practical to present the history of the Jews, which is so full of mysteries. The pastor will first teach

---

[33] . . . fidelium coniugia perfectione et nobilitate tum gentilium, tum Judaeorum matrimoniis longe praestare (II, 8, 22).

[34] . . . etsi Judaeis tantum videtur convenire . . . : tamen, si interiorem salutis universae rationem spectemus, multo magis ad Christianos homines pertinet . . . (III, 2, 1).

that God had chosen from all the peoples of the earth the one whose ancestor was Abraham."[35]

In concluding, it says "furthermore, the pastor should emphasize that there was but one nation which God chose from among all peoples, which He called chosen people, and by which He wanted to be known and worshiped."[36] This people was chosen by God expressly because Jesus Christ was to derive His human nature from that people.

The paragraph on matrimony mentions that "since the Jews had received the promise that all peoples would be blessed by a descendent of Abraham, they seemed to regard it their rightful, sacred duty to produce many offspring in order to carry on the successors of the chosen people, from which Christ the Lord was to receive His human nature."[37]

Let us now consider the Christological articles of the *Credo* in which reference is made to the Jews as a chosen people.

Second article: "And in Jesus Christ, His first born Son, our Lord." Supplementing the biblical passage, the catechism reads:

[35] . . . populi Israelitici historiam, quae mysteriorum est plena, diligenter explicare . . . ex omnibus nationibus . . . *unam* Deum delegisse (III, 1, 11).

[36] Ex his vero illud maxime parocho animadvertendum est: *unam* ex universis nationibus a Deo delectam esse, quam populum vocaret suum, et cui se cognoscendum et colendum praeberet (III, 1, 12).

[37] . . . filios procreare, electi populi sobolem, ex qua Christus Dominus Salvator noster, quod ad humanam naturam attinet, ortum habiturus esset, propagare . . . (II, 8, 18).

He will derive from Abraham who will bring salvation to all . . . according to the flesh born from the seed of Abraham" (I, 3, 4).

Jesus Christ is a son of the Jewish people (as shown in footnote 37). The name itself is of Jewish origin.

Many persons in Holy Scripture bear the name Jesus. Thus was called the son of Nave (Eccl. 46:1 ff.), the successor of Moses, who led the people liberated from Egypt by Moses into the Promised Land. That name also belonged to Josedech, the son of the high priest (Eccl. 49:12). But our Redeemer had a much greater right to this name—He who did not redeem a single people but the peoples of all times. . . . Thus we see Christ the Lord prefigured in those Old Testament persons who bore His name (I, 3, 6).

The name of Christ signifies prophet, priest and king. "The name of Prophet is His by the greatest right, inasmuch as all the prophets are but His disciples and had to have a Prophet proclaimed unto themselves. . . . Christ was at the same time a high priest—though not according to that order from which in the Old Testament only those of the tribe of Levi could be priests, but according to that of which the Prophet David cried: 'You are a priest forever according to the order of Melchisedech. . . .' We recognize Christ as our King. But He does not receive His kingdom by inheritance or some other human right, though He can trace His origin to kings of high renown" (I, 3, 7).

Third Article: "Who was conceived by the Holy Spirit, born of the Virgin Mary." Mary is of Jewish descent, and with her Christ also according to His human nature. "And now the magnificent promise made to Abraham would be fulfilled, to whom it was told that his progeny would bless all peoples. Mary, whom we truly honor and respect as the Mother of God, of Him who is both God and Man at the same time, traces her descent from King David" (I, 4, 7).[38]

A figure of the virgin birth is: "This gate of the temple shall be shut, it shall not be opened . . ." (Ezech. 44:2); and others: "Thus thou sawest, till a stone was cut out of a mountain without hands: and it struck the statue upon the feet thereof that were of iron and of clay, and broke them in pieces" (Dan. 2:34); ". . . the rod of Aaron for the house of Levi was budded" (IV Mos. 17:8); as well as the thornbush which Moses saw burning but "was not burnt" (II Mos. 3:2; I, 4, 10).

Fourth Article: "Who suffered under Pontius Pilate, was crucified, died and was buried." Here it states that "types of the passion and death of Christ are the sacrifice of Isaac, the lamb which the Jews slaughtered at the exodus from Egypt, and the serpent of brass in the desert" (I, 5, 5).

One fruit of the Savior's suffering is the opening of heaven. This too was prefigured in the Old Testament. "Certain Jews were not permitted to re-

---

[38] The Apostles, too, were designated "chosen" from the Jewish people (delectos ex Judaeorum populo, quales erant discipuli; II, 4, 24).

turn to the homeland until the death of the high priest (IV Mos. 35:25). Thus no one, however just and perfect his life, was able to enter the heavenly fatherland before the eternal high priest, Jesus Christ, had suffered His death" (I, 5, 14).

And who is to blame for the death of Jesus Christ? *Catechismus Romanus* does not speak in a generalizing way about the Jews who crucified Christ. Above all, together with Jews and Gentiles, the sinners assume responsibility for the crucifixion.

The catechism suggests a more exact paraphrasing of "under Pontius Pilate" which might read thus: "The prophesy of the Redeemer is fulfilled; they have delivered Him to the Gentiles for ridicule, torture and crucifixion" (I, 5, 3).

The sinners are to be blamed for the death of Christ more than the Jews, for "the sinners are instrumental in causing His suffering. . . . Those who wallow in sin and vice deride the Son of God and crucify Him all over again. This is a crime seemingly worse than that committed by the Jews" (I, 5, 11).

And in another place it says that "people from every walk of life and various social standing conspired against the Lord and His Son. Gentiles and Jews were the instigators of His sufferings and had carried out the sentence. Judas betrayed Him, Peter denied Him, and all abandoned Him" (I, 5, 13).

Fifth Article: "Descended into hell and on the

third day rose from the dead." Christ descended into purgatory where the souls of the saints were at rest before the arrival of Christ the Lord" (animae Sanctorum, I, 6, 3).

The reason given for the descent into Purgatory is that "He (Christ) desired to wrench the bounty from the devils, to liberate from prison the holy fathers and other pious people and lead them into heaven with Him" (santos illos Patres ceterosque pios e carcere liberatos, I, 5, 6).

Here, as in other parts of the catechism, it is clear that the patriarchs and fathers of prehistory are designated saints. It speaks of holy Fathers (sanctorum Patrum), meaning David and Isaias (II, 5, 23). In discussing the Sacrament of Matrimony, the example of the holy patriarchs is cited (sanctis illis patriarchis, II, 8, 13) so as to point out the desire for offspring as a motivation for matrimony. To illustrate the duties of parents toward their children, the catechism uses the beautiful example of Job, Tobias and the other holy Fathers (pulcherrima exempla Tobias, Job, et alii sanctissimi Patres, II, 8, 23). Christians pay tribute to the angels as did the saints of the Old Testament (exemplo sanctorum veteris Testamenti, III, 2, 8). And now a final quotation, the text on the Our Father prayer, namely, "And lead us not into temptation," includes a reference to the lives of "the holy men Adam, David and Salomon" (sanctorum hominum Adam, David, Salomon, IV, 15, 7).

Unfortunately, this opinion of *Catechismus Ro-*

manus that there are also saints among those of
the Old Testament as well as of the New has not
remained a valid truth in modern Christianity.[39]

> After the Jewish people was founded and its reli-
> gion established, the promise (that in the seed
> of Abraham all the people will be blessed) began
> to be known to His people. There were signs as
> well as prophecies that pointed to the great goods
> our Redeemer and Savior would bring to us. The
> prophets spoke before the people as any eyewit-
> ness might have done—and predicted the birth
> of the Son of God; the miraculous works which
> He would suffer; the resurrection, and all the
> other mysteries. Allowing only for the element of
> time there seems to be no difference between the
> prophecies of the prophets and the preachings of
> the Apostles, between the faith of the old patri-
> archs and our own faith."[40]

In both Testaments, from Moses and Paul respectively, we have ideal examples of how to pray
for the salvation of our neighbor.[41]

The catechism recognized the extensive use of
art in public and private devotion, inasmuch as
"one gets to know the history of both Testaments

[39] See the Martyrology; All Saints litany; matrimonial
blessing.

[40] . . . ut, si futuri et praeteriti temporis tollatur diversitas,
nihil iam inter Prophetarum praedicta et Apostolorum
praedicationem, nihil inter veterum Patriarcharum fidem et
nostram interesse videamus (I, 3, 4).

[41] . . . in utroque Testamento sanctorum Mosis et Pauli
(IV, 14, 16).

through sacred images, which refresh the memory
of divine things so as to love and worship God the
more."[42] Also, "it is the task of the lector to read
in church the books of the Old and the New Testaments."[43]

The above quotes will substantiate the intent of
Catechismus Romanus to establish a unity between
the Old and the New Testaments; the passages
from the Old are as frequent as those from the New.

Along with this view showing the unity of both
Testaments, the catechism stresses the fact that
the Old Testament was fulfilled by the coming of
Jesus. The New Testament has now replaced the
Old. The chosen people of God are now His Church.

IV. *The prayer of the Church of Christ for the conversion of the Jews.*

The preceding chapters of *Catechismus Romanus* treated the Jews as the chosen people of God,
as they had lived before Christ.[44] The concluding
part of this essay presents all the catechism references which treat the Jews as the living descendants of that people.[45]

[42] . . . ad utriusque Testamenti cognoscendam historiam
(III, 2, 24).
[43] . . . in ecclesia veteris et novi Testamenti libros . . .
recitare (II, 7, 16).
[44] *Catechismus Romanus* uses without distinction the
names of Jews, Hebrews and Israelites (as shown in III,
1, 11).
[45] At the time of Pius V the Jews in Rome were called
"Hebrews." See Pastor, *op. cit.*, 245. The Roman catechism
refers to them as Jews.

What does the Church, that people of God in the New Law, do for the conversion of these Jews?

The best and most impressive commentary is made in the fourth part of the catechism ("De Oratione"):

We must pray for all without exception and without regard to enmity, race or religion (IV, 5, 1)

According to the well-known testimony of St. Augustine (ep. 109), there exists a custom, handed down from the Apostles, of offering prayers and supplications on behalf of those who are separated from the Church: that the unbelievers may receive the gift of faith; that the idolators be freed from their errors; that the Jews accept the light of truth after the darkness of their hearts is illuminated; that the heretics return to truth and be reinstructed in the Catholic belief; that the schismatics be reunited through the link of love to Holy Mother Church whose community they have forsaken. The great effectiveness of such prayers, if offered in the right spirit, manifest itself in the example of the various people of all walks of life whom God rescues daily from the powers of evil and gives them the kingdom of His beloved Son, thus transforming the vessels of wrath into vessels of His mercy.[46]

---

[46] . . . ut Judaei discussa animorum caligine, lucem veritatis accipiant (IV, 5, 3). Compare the Good Friday prayer: ut, agnita veritatis tuae luce . . ., a suis tenebri eruantur.

In explaining the second line of the *Our Father,* "Thy kingdom come," there is again a commemoration of those separated from the Church:

We ask of God the spread of the kingdom of Christ, which is the Church, so that unbelievers and Jews may be converted to faith in Christ the Lord and knowledge of the true God, and that the schismatics and heretics return to truth and to community with the Church of God from which they have separated themselves.[47]

In order to understand the special significance of the above quotes we must consider them against the historical background. P. Browe says:

All through the Middle Ages, except in Spain, there were no other liturgical prayers in use, other than those on Good Friday, for the conversion of the Jews and the return of schismatics and heretics. It seems that the popes and bishops did little to admonish their people in that direction. . . . This would have been out of character in the Middle Ages; nor was it ever known that something similar had been done for the conversion of heretics and schismatics.[48]

In that area, *Catechismus Romanus* has intro-

[47] . . . ut se ad fidem Christi Domini et ad accipiendam veri Dei cognitionem convertant infideles et Judaei . . . (IV, 11, 12).

[48] Browe, *op. cit.,* 137. The quote between parenthesis is not a literal one.

duced a definite change. This catechism, which recognizes the only chosen people as being the Church, does not ignore those outside the fold but wants them to find the true way.

It is noteworthy that in the above quotes the Jews are always mentioned together with the unbelivers, schismatics and heretics. And again, when the subject of baptism is treated, Jews, unbelievers, heretics and schismatics are named together, i.e., "In cases of emergency, Jews, unbelievers, and heretics may baptize."[49]

When it comes to choosing sponsors, the catechism warns that "Jews, heretics and unbelievers should be kept away from such an office, because they generally resort to lies and schemes in order to distort the truth and destroy Christian piety."[50]

Another point that attracts our attention is the fact that, wherever Jews and unbelievers are named together, the Jews are put either immediately before or right after the infidels. Evidently the authors seem to consider the Jews on a level with the infidels.

In presenting the article of faith concerning the Church, where the three classes of people are listed as being excluded from the community, the Jews are not at all included. "The above shows that only three categories of men are excluded from the Church: first, the unbelievers; then the heretics

[49] Nam et Judaeis quoque, infidelibus et haereticis . . (II, 2, 24).

[50] . . . haeretici in primis, Judaei, infideles ab hoc munere omnino prohibendi sunt (II, 2, 29).

and schismatics; and finally those who are excommunicated."[51]

Once more, in the ninth article of faith, mention is made of the unbelieving Jews in regard to Christianity. It is cited that "everyone can understand by reason and perceive with his senses that there is a Church, a community of men on earth who are devoted to Christ the Lord and dedicated to Him; to understand this, faith is not necessary since neither Jews nor Turks doubt it."[52]

Here, of course, it is possible to track this down to the Middle Ages, at which time the Jews were known to be the sole unbelievers in the midst of a purely Christian world. Only in Spain and southern Italy did the Jews, together with the Mohammedans, pass for "infidels."[53]

The stipulation resulting from the Council of Agde, namely, that the catechumens be subjected to an especially long period of preparation (see footnotes 9 and 10), is also cited in the *Catechismus Romanus* as the ideal way to test the true intentions of the candidates. No longer is it a condition applying only to the Jews.[54]

[51] Ex quo fit, ut tria tatcummodo hominum genera ab ea excludantur: primo infideles, deinde haeretici et schismatici, postremo excommunicati (I, 10, 9).

[52] . . . neque ad eam rem animo concipiendam fide opus esse videatur, quum nec Judaei, nec Turcae quidem de eo dubitent (I, 10, 20).

[53] See W. Neuss, "Die Kirche und das Judentum in der Geschichte," *Beiträge zur Christlichen Betrachtung der Judenfrage* (Freiburg i. Br., 1951), 18, 32.

[54] Cuius rei causa in antiquis conciliis decretum legimus, ut qui ex Judaeis ad fidem catholicam veniunt . . . (II, 2, 36).

Another example from the early Church's baptismal procedure is effectively used to point out that baptism remits all punishment for sin. Therefore the neophyte should not be burdened with excessive preparations:

The custom of the Old Church which prescribed a forty-day fast for the neophytes is not contrary to this. The requirement was not meant to be an atonement, but an admonishment for neophytes to fast and pray for a while without interruption out of respect for the dignity of the sacrament.[55]

Will the Jewish people some day be converted? What does the *Catechismus Romanus* say about it? Pius V had expelled from the Papal States those Jews who did not want to be converted. Among the themes of the sermons projected toward the conversion of the Jews was, oddly enough, the rejection of Israel. It is in vain that we are looking for a hint of the rejection of the Jew in *Catechismus Romanus*.[56] Nor do we find any allusion to the salvation of the Jews at the end of the world, as Paul states it (Rom. 11:26). Rather than make such

[55] Nec vero, quae hoc loco traduntur, veteris ecclesiae consuetudini adversantur, quae olim Judaeis, quum baptizarentur, praecipiebat, ut quadraginta continuos dies ieunarent (II, 2, 45).

[56] St. Paul's words, "For I wished myself to be an anathema from Christ, for my brethren, who are kinsmen according to the flesh" (Rom. 9:3), as well as the prayer of Moses in the Old Testament (Exod. 32:31 f.), may be cited here to explain the phrase "Forgive us" in the Our Father prayer—thus illustrating that we should pray for the salvation of our neighbor (IV, 14, 16).

an allusion, the catechism merely notes that "as a sign preceding the Last Judgment, Holy Scripture mentions these above all: the proclamation of the gospel over the whole earth, apostasy, and the advent of the Antichrist."[57]

The *Catechismus Romanus* neither rejects the Jewish people nor upholds them as the elected people of God. It considers only one chosen people of God, and that is the Church. Outside of the Church there is no other chosen people. The Synagogue was a type (figura) of the Church; and where the City of Jerusalem is again named as a type, it is explained in such a way that the exclusive character of the Church is proved (see footnote 26). When explaining the unity of the Church, St. Jerome is quoted (Letter 15, 2 to Damasus): "I know that the Church is built on that rock (Peter). He who eats the lamb outside this house is unholy."[58]

The question posed at the beginning of this chapter, that is, how the *Catechismus Romanus* treated the question of the Jews, has been answered. Should we want to quote the catechism on this question, we could not find a better answer than the expression by Dyonisius, whose reference to divine action (divinitus) has been given by the authors of the catechism: "Our Church is standing in the middle between the Synagogue and the divine Jerusalem and therefore partakes of both."[59]

[57] . . . praedicationem evangelii per universum orbem, discessionem, Antichristum . . . (I, 8, 7).

[58] Quinquunque extra hanc domum agnum comederit, profanus est (I, 10, 12).

[59] Cf. fn. 28.